D0953087

the bloody mary

the bloody mary

THE LORE AND LEGEND OF A COCKTAIL CLASSIC, WITH RECIPES FOR BRUNCH AND BEYOND

brian bartels

PHOTOGRAPHY BY
Eric Medsker

ILLUSTRATIONS BY
Ruby Taylor

TEN SPEED PRESS
California | New York

This book is dedicated to my grandfather Roland Bartels, who taught me inspiration; to my family and friends, who teach me about love and music; and to all bartenders and service professionals everywhere.

The world is our crossword, and there is no hidden meaning for one simple clue: Engage.

contents

recipe list

introduction

Before we begin, I have a confession: I used to be skeptical of the legendary drink we know as the Bloody Mary. I was a scrawny little wisenheimer, just out of college and living in Madison, Wisconsin. When it came to day drinking, I was a steadfast beer man. Beer was fast, simple, and it made me feel ten years older than my dumb youth. Yet every Saturday and Sunday morning, when I arrived at my bartending gig at the Great Dane brewpub, the Bloody Mary was there waiting for me: red and soupy, viscous and spicy.

Wisconsinites are thirsty and wonderful people. We greet each day with a celebratory joie de vivre—and Friday is no exception. This often means that our Saturday starts with a Bloody. In a bar, there are probably more Bloody Marys made and ordered on a Saturday than the six other days combined. During my early days as a bartender, I had to learn how to be creative and fast on the busiest Bloody day of the week. I soon discovered that a bartender can't make drinks fast enough in a college town. And so my complicated relationship with the Bloody Mary began.

I've been behind the stick for nearly twenty years, most recently as beverage director of Gabriel Stulman's Happy Cooking Hospitality group's restaurants: Joseph Leonard, Jeffrey's Grocery, Fedora, Perla Cafe, and Bar Sardine, all in New York City's Greenwich Village. Our restaurants celebrate the spirit of communal dining, so it's no surprise that the most convivial of cocktails, the Bloody Mary, plays a key role. We have built a reputation for being a great venue for (often Bloody Mary–fueled) neighborhood get-togethers, and as such, we are constantly working to develop, sustain, and improve the Happy Cooking Bloody Mary portfolio.

But that doesn't mean I've forgotten where it all began: the untamable brunch service at the Great Dane, my first scheduled shift as a bartender.

Every Saturday morning, I'd enter work—hungover, sleep-deprived—and fumble with ingredients while my manager and fellow bartenders snickered at my inexperienced, gawky attempts to impress. My reflexes were still adjusting to unfamiliar movements like shaking cocktails, pouring the perfect pint, and cutting bottomless buckets of lemons and limes without slicing my finger off. No matter what I did, I was too slow. I felt like I was learning how to fly-fish in a kayak in torrential rains. But I was determined to do well; I was the new guy, and I had to learn technique and etiquette before I could graduate to the nobler night shift (and the privilege of sleeping in after working [and drinking] Wednesday, Thursday, and Friday nights). The Bloody Mary was the gatekeeper; it was the sphinx that guarded the entrance to the world of bartending. To move forward, I had to master the Bloody—and unlock its mysteries.

The first thing I learned was that a very specific social climate forms wherever Bloody Marys are poured. I've seen drinkers, wild-eyed, ravenous, and possibly still a touch inebriated from the previous evening, detour from important appointments just to have one. I have seen devotees park outside closed restaurant doors, tapping their feet and champing at the bit to get inside and order the sacred libation, then spend an entire morning and afternoon nursing them. The Bloody is not a drink one sucks down, vacuumlike. It is not a shot. It's an esteemed cocktail that commands patience.

The Bloody Mary also taught me that everyone is unique. Bloody Mary bartenders and drinkers all enjoy "the tweak," as I like to call it—adding an extra dash of Tabasco, a splash of crisp lager, or an extra olive (or six).

Learning to make a great Bloody Mary also taught me about survival. Its restorative power is unmatched in the cocktail world—and I felt powerful, too, handing a Bloody to a tattered, shaky-handed customer, then watching as they rose, phoenixlike, from the ashes of the night before. All it takes is a few sips. For the more restrained and health-conscious among us, we enjoy a Bloody for its antioxidants, nutrients, and electrolytes. Or simply for the fortifying conversation it inspires. The Bloody Mary is very much a public cocktail. The over-the-top garnishes turn heads when a Bloody enters a room. It gets people talking.

"Where's yours?" is the most common refrain in any Bloody Mary–related conversation. The first one arrives, and the person drinking glances around to see who else will partake, to see who else will join him or her on the long, hard road to recovery. It's no surprise, then, that the Bloody Mary thrives in and around barbecues and picnics, tailgates, breakfast and brunch hotspots, airports, train stations, golf courses, book groups, or wherever people are getting ready to seize the day.

To this day, no other cocktail has achieved as much notoriety as the Bloody Mary. The stakes are high when you order a Bloody, which might explain why many bartenders (including my youthful self) sigh when they hear you ask for one. But in fact, the Bloody Mary is an opportunity for any bartender, amateur or professional, to show off their best selves: the affable and engaging party host, a medical practitioner eager to heal, an artist with a blank canvas. And really, we should welcome any reason to take a moment to catch up on life; to possibly gain some much-needed clarity on what happened in the past twelve to twenty-four hours; to ask the important questions, such as where are my keys, phone, and pants. Ever the social butterfly, the Bloody Mary bridges the gaps among us all.

Where's yours?

BACON?

Yep.

CELERY?

Always.

BARBECUE CAYENNE SHRIMP?

Sure.

PICKLED EGG, LANDJÄGER & A CHUNK OF JALAPEÑO CHEDDAR?

Are you kidding me? Cancel your plans!

what's in a bloody mary?

Cocktail fashions come and go, but the nourishing charm of a Bloody Mary endures. The Bloody Mary pushes boundaries while staying true to its roots. Over the course of its eighty-year history, its garnishes have stretched all across the culinary map.

A classic Bloody Mary contains the following ingredients: tomato juice, vodka, spices, and seasonings. It often includes Worcestershire sauce, lemon juice, black pepper, celery salt, and a curveball ingredient that is generally left up to the creator. As with any well-made cocktail, a Bloody Mary should be balanced, but that curveball ingredient should also make the drink fun, inspiring good-to-the-last-drop smiles.

When I first started making Bloody Marys, in my early twenties, I would add lemon and lime juices, olives, pickle brine, Worcestershire, and Tabasco, and then I would pop an ounce of Guinness in at the end, a little luck o' the Irish for a finale. People commented on how much they enjoyed the recipe, but I didn't think it was rewriting history or anything like that. My Bloody was great because it was consistent.

To make a Bloody Mary unforgettable, one doesn't need the flair of a master mixologist or the prowess of a celebrity chef. A level of consistency is a sound barometer. The true fabric of what goes into a Bloody Mary will vary from recipe to recipe. Think of it this way: there are few cocktails that allow you to sub in every spirit under the sun! Personally, I think a sound Bloody should include tomato juice, vodka, black pepper, salt, Worcestershire sauce, spices, and lemon juice. While some of those ingredients can be altered or substituted, the only variable I feel has no substitute is temperature. I like my Bloody Marys served chilled or with ice.

I wanted this book to have a healthy variety of Bloody Mary options, which is why we have recipes that approach the classic cocktail in myriad ways. Some recipes call for variations on the base ingredients, such as Aquavit replacing vodka (that would be a Danish Mary, page 111) or carrot juice standing in for tomato juice (pages 72, 102, and 116). And, of course, there are classic recipes included within these pages, as they deserve recognition for trailblazing the way for so many variations. We Bloody Mary connoisseurs are nothing if not experimental. We like to agitate the norms. "Logic will get you from A to Z," says Albert Einstein. "Imagination will get you everywhere else."

the history of the bloody mary

The good news is, the Bloody Mary was invented. Let that be reassurance in difficult times, when you're navigating the spice-laden, red sea of life.

The answer to the question of how it originated, however, is a murky one. There is lots of speculation surrounding the history of one of the world's most famous cocktails, who invented it, and when.

Before the Bloody Mary ever came into being, hungover Americans of the nineteenth century were known to enjoy the Oyster cocktail, which, to my mind, is a calamity of a drink: you crack one egg into a glass, douse it with seasoning spices and Worcestershire sauce or vinegar, and down it in one gulp. To me, that sounds like a recipe for broken egg yolks, spilled spices, oily fingers, and possibly even a cursing spouse or roommate. If one didn't feel better in its aftermath, moaning and groaning out loud may have eventually alleviated the symptoms.

Then something wonderful happened in the early twentieth century: people started developing palates. And so, food and drink began to evolve and grow in wonderful ways. The 1920s was a decade of cultural progress: think jazz, Art Deco, and the Lost Generation, the group of writers who popularized many of the cocktails we drink and toast with today. And let's not forget that Prohibition was in effect throughout the 1920s.

Let me repeat the critical word in that last paragraph: Prohibition. As in, no liquor—and no fun! It's a miracle we made it to the mid-1930s and lived to tell the tale.

Prohibition made it difficult for Americans to consume alcoholic beverages from 1920 to 1933. During those thirteen years, people who could afford a ticket by boat or plane traveled abroad to reap the reward of cultural expansion, in the form of legal liquor and legal fun.

Bars in Europe and Cuba saw some interesting expats during those times— both bartenders and patrons. The New York Bar in Paris, France, was one such haven. Owned and operated in the early 1920s by an American former jockey named Tod Sloan, the New York Bar in Paris served alcoholic beverages to many a United States serviceman stationed in France during and after World War I.

Due to personal gambling issues, Sloan was forced to sell the New York Bar in 1923 to one of his bartenders, a Scotsman named Harry McElhone, who then renamed the establishment Harry's New York Bar.

Ask any well-read modern mixologist about Harry's New York Bar, and there's a good chance they'll speak about it so excitedly, it'll seem as if they've been there. Harry's became a destination for Americans and expats during Prohibition, even hosting the likes of Hemingway and a slew of post–World War I writers and artists, such as F. Scott Fitzgerald, George Gershwin, and Coco Chanel. Part of its sustained allure points to Harry's being the birthplace of such famous cocktails as the French 75, the sidecar, and, ostensibly, the Bloody Mary.

Popular Bloody Mary legend points to Fernand "Pete" Petiot, a bartender at Harry's New York Bar in the 1920s, as a possible creator of our titular drink. Vodka was common enough in France, and the tomato juice cocktail—a combination of pressed tomato juice and vodka with a dash of lemon—was gaining traction. Petiot started at the bar as a kitchen boy in 1916, only sixteen years old at the time, and worked his way up to bartender. While the First World War was taking place, Petiot assisted American soldiers as their unofficial banker, holding their military pay for allocated bar tabs and cash to wire home. I can only imagine what it was like to bartend a busy bar with Ernest Hemingway yelling drink orders to me while soldiers are waiting for me to get them twenty dollars from the safe.

Harry's popularity had much to do with that fact that young Petiot was behind the stick. There is no question that Petiot was front and center during a creative renaissance happening in the cocktail world, and his ability to engage and uncover new frontiers elevated his status in the bar world. Working as a kitchen staffer at Harry's for six years before becoming a bartender helped Petiot establish trust and loyalty with the regulars; the hallowed position of bartender only heightened Petiot's steadfast integrity at his workplace. He may have even taken over bartending for Harry himself, and legend has it, Petiot owns a beer-drinking record at the famous bar. When not making grasshoppers and stingers for the masses, he claimed to make a drink for American expats that consisted of tomato juice and vodka—but he called it the Bloody Mary while at Harry's Bar it wasn't popular enough to catch on in print.

The first nonalcoholic tomato juice cocktail can be traced to 1917 in French Lick, Indiana, where, one morning, a French chef working at a resort and spa couldn't find oranges to make orange juice. Instead, he grabbed a handful of tomatoes, squeezed them, and added sugar. That version of the tomato juice cocktail made its way to Chicago shortly thereafter, and freshly squeezed tomato juice started trending in the early 1920s.

Some people doubt of Petiot's claim that he created the alcoholic tomato juice cocktail. It's a gray area, as nonalcoholic versions started appearing everywhere in the 1920s, with strained tomato juice, Worcestershire sauce, and spices, but no one claims to have invented that particular recipe. It is suspect, for example, that Harry McElhone published a book of bar recipes in 1927 called *Barflies and Cocktails*, yet there is no tomato juice–vodka recipe in its three hundred recipes. If Petiot was indeed serving Papa Hemingway Bloodys at Harry's, wouldn't McElhone have written about it in his book?

REFLECTIONS ON THE ALMIGHTY HANGOVER

A hangover is what happens when alcohol and your body pick a fight on the adult playground we call life. The body is missing some vitamin B, diminishing mental and muscular continuity, which can often feel like trying to swim through an Olympic-size pool of peanut butter. Everyone has a different response to treating the almighty hangover. Some sip on coconut water, others eat a banana. Some people head to the gym, a few do yoga, and others hit up a sauna or steam bath if they're lucky enough to have one nearby.

One of my favorite tips on fighting hangovers comes from 1949's *Esquire's Handbook for Hosts,* tip no. 3:

"Upon arising, try to force yourself to do a little mild exercising—or, if that seems impossible, stand at the open window and breathe deeply as many times as you can stand it."

Of course, the best way to avoid a hangover is to *not* drink. Or you could hold a crown of parsley over your head, which is what they used to do in Greece. For your precautionary pleasure, I've included nonalcoholic Bloody Mary variations, such as the the Red Wagon (page 106) and Mary on Holiday (page 80), but know you can omit alcohol from any of these recipes. We've all been down the road when good judgment gets the best of us. Sometimes it's nice to opt for some preventive and still delicious alternatives.

What's more, commercial tomato juice wasn't invented and mass-produced until the late 1920s, so it's safe to say the Bloody Mary wasn't available until the mid-1930s, or post-Prohibition. College Inn Tomato Factory debuted canned tomato juice in the United States in 1928. The popularity of canned tomato juice, marketed as "tomato juice cocktail," escalated over the next five years, perhaps thanks to slogans such as this:

> *Delicious, rich, pre-seasoned. Before or between meal treat.*
> *JUST RIGHT morning, noon, and night. Come on—Taste it!"*

Here's a 1931 quote from a print ad for College Inn, featuring Broadway and movie star Genevieve Tobin:

> *"I have found that College Inn Tomato Juice Cocktails are not only a refreshing drink, but a fine health tonic. I keep several bottles on ice and enjoy a modest full tumbler with each meal."*
>
> *—Sincerely, Genevieve Tobin, Universal Star*

In his autobiography, *The World I Lived In*, New York comedian George Jessel claimed he invented a tomato juice, Worcestershire sauce, and vodka cocktail in 1927 after an all-night drinking session. Still awake, nursing a righteous 8:00 a.m. hangover, and uncertain of what to drink at La Maze, then a popular restaurant in Palm Beach, Florida, Jessel claims to have been inspired when someone produced a bottle of potato vodka (called vodkee at the time, as it had a rotten potato aroma). However, some are skeptical of Jessel's story—canned tomato juice was not yet invented, so where was he getting the tomato juice to mix with the seasonings, spices, and mystery bottle of vodka?

The third plausible origin story involves Henry Zbikiewicz, a bartender at New York City's esteemed 21 Club, who is known for combining tomato juice and vodka at the bar in the 1930s. But was he the *originator* of the practice? (Jessel, it should be noted, also frequented the 21 Club in the early 1930s, so it's entirely possible that the recipe landed on Zbikiewicz's lap via Jessel.)

But in a 1982 *New York Times* article, Zbikiewicz gives Jessel credit for the Henry Morgan and Vodka Southside cocktails, yet doesn't mention the Bloody Mary, leaving that origin unsubstantiated.

But let's not give up on our favorite Frenchman, Fernand Petiot, just yet. In 1933, Petiot left Paris for post-Prohibition New York City and a bartending gig at the St. Regis Hotel's celebrated King Cole Bar. He had a staff of seventeen barmen working for him, who saw him as the godfather of cocktails. After all, during the 1920s, Petiot had mastered his skills overseas while the rest of America was slowly forgetting how to mix drinks. Petiot raised the quality and execution of cocktails at the bar, establishing standards that bartenders maintain even today. He met each shift with an open mind and approached the trade as though it were something he could always improve upon, which is why he is referred to as a master bartender.

One of the first post-Prohibition drinks Petiot introduced on the King Cole Bar menu was the Red Snapper—a combination of vodka, tomato juice, citrus, and spices, which may also have included a seasoning called Red Snapper. Produced by J.G. Fox and Co. in the Pacific Northwest, the mix contained fresh clams, spices, and tomatoes; the label warned that it was "highly concentrated hot." An overnight sensation, the Red Snapper made its debut in Crosby Gaige's 1941 *Cocktail Guide and Ladies' Companion*.

Originally, Petiot wanted to call his new cocktail the Bloody Mary, but Vincent Astor, son of John Jacob Astor IV and owner of the St. Regis, deemed the name too offensive for his clientele (it probably didn't help Mr. Astor was married to his second wife, a woman named Mary, around this time). Could it be that two different rabbit holes would lead to the same destination? Could the Red Snapper be our beloved Bloody Mary, parading under a different name?

Whoa. So while it didn't go by its now-famous name, there is good cause to believe that Petiot is responsible for creating the cayenne, lemon, black pepper, Worcestershire sauce, tomato, and vodka cocktail we know today.

I drink too much. The last time I gave a urine sample it had an olive in it.

—RODNEY DANGERFIELD

When life throws tomatoes at you, make Bloody Marys.

—GREETING CARD

Every golfer will appreciate that it is very necessary for getting one out of the "rough."

—EDDIE CLARKE, *SHAKING IN THE 60'S*, 1963

If you just go by the printed record, however, it would seem as if Jessel were the originator: he gets credit for name-dropping the Bloody Mary in print for the first time, in a column by the epicurean and bon vivant Lucius Beebe in the *New York Herald Tribune* in December 1939 (Jessel called the Bloody Mary "the newest pick-me-up"). Then, in a *Collier's* advertisement for Smirnoff from March 1956, Jessel declares, "I *think* I invented the Bloody Mary, Red Snapper, Tomato Pickup, or Morning Glory. It happened on a night before a day and I felt I should take some good, nourishing tomato juice, but what I really wanted was some of your good Smirnoff Vodka. So I mixed them together, the juice for the body and the vodka for the spirit, and if I wasn't the first ever, I was the happiest ever."

But, for me, the most important piece of evidence is this quote from a *New Yorker* interview with Petiot from July 18, 1964. Petiot was asked about his legacy as a heralded New York barman and offered these closing remarks:

> "*I initiated the Bloody Mary of today. George Jessel said he created it, but it was really nothing but vodka and tomato juice when I took it over. I cover the bottom of the shaker with four large dashes of salt, two dashes of black pepper, two dashes of cayenne pepper, and a layer of Worcestershire sauce; I then add a dash of lemon juice and some cracked ice, put in two ounces of vodka and two ounces of thick tomato juice, shake, strain, and pour. We make a hundred to a hundred and fifty Bloody Marys a day here in the King Cole Room and in the other restaurants and the banquet rooms.*"

To me, this is the most plausible origin story. Jessel takes credit for the combination of vodka, Worcestershire sauce, and tomato juice, and Petiot modernized it with spices and seasoning. I am satisfied with the idea that George Jessel created the name (see Mary Theory No. 3, page 19) and early version of the drink, while Petiot crafted it into the version of the cocktail we think of today. Jessel's campaigning with Smirnoff in the 1950s gave rise to its prominence, while Petiot's refinements created a benchmark for countless variations.

THE NAME

What is in a name? As it turns out, a healthy amount of speculation. While one might assume that the eponym for this notable beverage would have a statue on some mountaintop somewhere (I can see it now: she's waving a flag in one hand and sipping from a large red goblet filled with celery, carrots, bacon, olives, pickles, and mirth in the other), in fact, no one knows who the true inspiration for the name of this drink really is. There are four predominant theories, though, which I outline below.

---

mary theory no. 1

The Bloody Mary is named for Queen Mary Tudor of England.

One thing is for certain, Queen Mary Tudor was a stone-cold Catholic badass. She ruled over England and Ireland in the sixteenth century, and, well, we're lucky the drink isn't called Raining Down Hellfire Mary, as the infamous queen took no prisoners. Queen Mary earned the nickname of Bloody Mary after reinstituting the Heresy Acts of 1554, through which she persecuted nearly three hundred Protestants for being rabble-rousers, sentencing most of them to death by fire. While Mary Tudor is certainly the most famous person to be called Bloody Mary, to my mind, there has never been enough evidence linking the queen to the cocktail.

mary theory no. 2

The Bloody Mary is named for a waitress named Mary from the historic saloon Bucket of Blood in Chicago.

The New Delaware bar went by a famous nickname: the Bucket of Blood. It operated in Chicago in the early nineteenth century and was so named for the stabbings, bar fights, and brawls that took place nearly every night. When they mopped the floor at closing . . . you get the idea. No need to be graphic. On Sean Parnell's website, the Chicago Bar Project, he quotes a *Chicago Tribune* article from February 25, 1916: "It is a small, dark, sordid, dismal place, and we couldn't stand it very long."

Some sources suggest that Petiot got his naming inspiration from a Bucket of Blood regular who was drinking at the St. Regis one night; the unnamed regular mentioned a Bucket of Blood waitress, Mary, and the rest is history. The story is feasible, but there isn't enough evidence to support it.

mary theory no. 3

The Bloody Mary is named for Mary of New York's St. Regis Hotel.

This Mary theory rarely surfaces, but it's intriguing. Legend has it a woman named Mary frequented Petiot's bar, sitting by her lonesome, forever waiting on a gentleman who never materialized. Petiot and his colleagues began referring to her as Mary, Queen of Scots, the renowned monarch condemned to solitary captivity, forever unable to escape confinement. This is by far the most romantic—albeit ill-fated—version of the story, if only it would hold up. Imagine a drink being named after you as you waited among a sea of strangers. Imagine being the strong-willed woman who said "F*** that guy!" and decided to keep on drinking at the bar, no matter what anyone else says or thinks, taking a flamethrower to the social conventions dictating that a woman shouldn't drink unchaperoned. Like. A. Boss. It's Romeo and Juliet without the Romeo. (#girlpower)

I introduced the Bloody Mary to Hong Kong in 1941 and believe it did more than any other single factor except perhaps the Japanese Army to precipitate the fall of that Crown Colony.

—ERNEST HEMINGWAY

mary theory no. 4

The Bloody Mary is named for Mary Brown Warburton, a socialite who was George Jessel's friend.

In George Jessel's autobiography, he describes the supposed birthday of the Bloody Mary at the Florida restaurant La Maze in 1927. Charlie, a La Maze bartender, offered the hungover patrons a dusty bottle he called vodkee. Seeing as it was seven years into Prohibition, most had never seen the "rotten potato smelling" spirit, as vodka—along with bars and bartenders—was highly uncommon during 1920s Prohibition. Embracing the moment, Jessel mixed the contraband with Worcestershire sauce, tomato juice, and lemon. After a few sips, everyone started to feel better.

Shortly thereafter, bon vivant and socialite Mary Brown Warburton arrived, still wearing her white evening gown from the night before. When Jessel gave her the newly concocted drink, she conveniently spilled the beverage on her dress. "Now you can call me Bloody Mary, George!" Mary said, laughing it off.

Despite the fact that it involves the memories of a man who, by his own admission, had just wrapped up an all-night drinking binge, I find this theory the most credible. Jessel emphatically reiterated the story in many different publications in the decades that followed.

Years later, Jessel recalled working a benefit with entertainer Ted Healy, who was, as was his custom, slightly inebriated. Before they were scheduled to entertain that night's audience, Healy picked up a Chicago newspaper and read Walter Winchell's column, which stated that Jessel named the drink after Mary Warburton, Ted Healy's girlfriend at the time Jessel claimed to have created the drink.

"What the hell are you doing making a pass at my girl, you son of a bitch!" Healy yelled. Jessel claims Healy pulled out a pistol and tried to shoot him. Jessel ducked and the shot missed him, but, as the pistol went off right next to Jessel's ear, he went deaf for a week. "I had a hell of a time doing the benefit that night," said Jessel in his memoir.

WISCONSIN

✪	State Capital	◉	County Seats
	State Boundary		County Boundary
	Railroads	90 12	Main Highways
◉	State Parks		

SCALE, 7¼ Miles to the Inch

0   10   20   30   40

LAND ELEVATIONS

Over 1,800 Feet Above Sea Level

From 1,500 to 1,800 Feet

From 1,200 to 1,500 Feet

From 1,000 to 1,200 Feet

From 800 to 1,000 Feet

From 581 to 800 Feet

Published by A. J. NYSTROM & CO., Chicago

the home bar(tender)

Nothing feels better than hosting friends in the comfort of one's residence. The home bar should be viewed as a rendezvous, a sanctuary from so much hullabaloo occurring in the outside world, a space to congregate and share time, stories, and yes, a proper drink or two.

Anyone who has ever attended an afternoon party, a bridal or baby shower, a family get-together, a holiday feast, and so on, has experienced the interaction a Bloody Mary station inspires. My parents often hosted get-togethers with our neighbors and friends, and before too long bottles of liquor would appear on a regal towel draped over our kitchen table. A makeshift bar with the necessary mixers was always stationed nearby, with two-liter bottles of cola, 7Up, and mini bottles of tonic water and club soda adorning the spread. I was allowed to eat as many pretzels and drink as much soda pop as my little Bartels belly could handle.

There were garnishes for the drinks: olives, cocktail onions, pickles, lemons, and lime slices. Cheese, crackers, breadsticks, carrots, and celery festooned the relish tray. Adults arrived, offering handshakes and hugs, coats were taken, and before taking their seats, guests would make themselves a drink. I recall bouncing around each room, unable to contain my excitement. I was high on the social buzz and convivial spirit—or maybe it was the liter of RC Cola in my bloodstream.

I observed the adults pouring funny-smelling liquids from exotic bottles into elegant glassware, curious about what was going on before my eyes. It's no surprise us kids were fascinated by how the adults built their cocktails; the drinks were like Legos, and there was no better Lego castle than the Bloody Mary. It wasn't just a straw or a lemon wedge. It was freshly ground black pepper. Salt. Worcestershire sauce. A celery stalk. And then an olive or three. Depending on the artist at work, there may have even been horseradish, shoveled in with a long-handled spoon.

We witnessed ingredients coming out of nowhere—all of them going into the same glass. When would it stop? Did Aunt Joanie just dip a chunk of summer sausage into her drink? Did Mr. Olsen add olive brine? They kept opening the refrigerator and looking back at the glass. What else could happen? To *just one cocktail?!*

But always, insistently and triumphantly, as though the creator had just ascended an undiscovered mountain and wished to claim it as their own, the Bloody Mary was finished with a pickle.

No wonder noted cocktail author and spirits historian Robert Hess calls it the meatloaf of the cocktail world.

tools and techniques

There are a few essential tools and ingredients that should be in any home bar setup, but the Bloody Mary station should also show off the host's creativity and personality. Creative cocktails are noble ways of breaking the ice and will add to the success of your party.

Here are the necessities for hosting a proper Bloody Mary party:

1. **Space.** Don't tuck the bartender in some dark, tiny corner. Find a central but unobtrusive spot where you can attractively lay out your tools and ingredients. There should be plenty of elbow room to cut or juice citrus and operate a shaker.

The Bloody Mary is like a backyard barbecue. Everyone thinks his is the best.

—DALE DEGROFF

Perhaps the most beautiful thing about the Bloody Mary is the fact that she keeps reinventing herself. The Bloody Mary is the Madonna of the cocktail world.

—JACK MCGARRY, FROM *DIFFORD'S GUIDE*

2. **Plumbing.** Is there a sink with hot and cold water close to the bar? Hopefully. This isn't a deal breaker, but it certainly helps to clean your barware as you go, so as not to leave behind a mess of shakers and glasses.

3. **Ice.** Ah yes, that sweet cold bastion of temperature-friendly consistency. Ice is necessary and, without a doubt, a priority when hosting a party. If the freezer is full of tomatoes you're readying for tomato water (see page 75), consider using a cooler or wine bucket for ice storage. Replenish with backup ice from another part of the house. A solid rule is to have a half pound of ice for each guest.

   If you're using cracked "party ice" from a grocery store, note that it melts more quickly than cubed ice and might dilute the cocktail, leading it to be imbalanced or watery. Strain any excess water and use a larger quantity of the smaller pieces of ice, then stir, roll, or agitate the shaker for less time.

4. **Towels.** The Bloody Mary will go down in history as one of the messiest cocktails ever made, so it's only fitting we include towels here. Use something absorbent that you're not afraid to get dirty.

5. **Barware.** There's no need to MacGyver a cocktail setup with an egg whisk and that extra pair of shoelaces you've had for years. Just have the right tools at the ready.

   - **Glassware.** Pint glasses are sturdy and the standard for serving Bloodys, but you can use just about any glass: rocks, goblet, sling (a footed 10-ounce glass), highball (a tall 8- to 10-ounce glass), or hurricane (a footed glass as big as 20 ounces) all work well.

   - **Pitcher.** A 64-ounce pitcher can hold enough Bloodys to serve 8 to 10 ice-filled pint glasses.

   - **Mixing glass.** Only some of the recipes in this book are stirred—most are rolled in a cocktail shaker. For stirred drinks, A 16- or 20-ounce pint glass is ideal. If you'd *really* like to impress your guests, seek out a 500 ml Yarai mixing glass from Cocktail Kingdom. Hubba hubba!

   - **Shaker.** I recommend a stainless steel Boston shaker, consisting of two interlocking "tins," for rolling or mixing the cocktails. (Alternatively, you can use a shaker with one metal tin and one glass.) As long as you develop a flair for the roll technique (see page 34), you'll be all set. Shoot for the moon.

- **Juicer.** A handheld juicer for limes, lemons, and other citrus will make your life so much easier. Remember, you will always extract more juice from room-temperature citrus. For more advanced fruit and vegetable juices, such as celery, cucumber, and pineapple, I recommend an industrial commercial juicer, such as Breville, Waring, or Nutrifaster.
- **Wide strainer and a funnel.** If you're building a big Bloody batch, a wide, fine-mesh strainer can help.
- **Hawthorne strainer.** Though it may not be necessary for Bloody Mary bars, the Hawthorne strainer looks important. The metal, two-pronged cocktail strainer has a metal spring designed to fit inside the rim of your shaker or mixing glass. If it buys you some smoke and mirrors, roll with one or two—always keep 'em guessing.
- **Muddler.** A helpful bartending tool, muddlers are great for cracking ice; extracting oils from fresh herbs such as mint, sage, or basil; and bruising cucumber. I don't recommend wooden muddlers, as they tend to chip and summon bacteria; it's best to use a plastic or steel muddler with a flat bottom. Let's see those elbows at work, sexy!
- **Drinking straws.** Not essential, but it always helps to have them so mama doesn't ruin her lipstick.
- **Garnish skewers.** Best to source both short and long skewers, depending on the depth and number of your garnishes.
- **Knives.** Both a paring knife and a serrated knife are useful tools. Serrated knives will cut fruit wedges far more easily, and paring knives are unbeatable with zesting and slicing citrus peels and other garnishes.
- **Cutting board.** A flat, easy-to-wash work surface is especially necessary if you're constantly replenishing your garnishes.
- **Barspoon.** Ideally, this should be 10 to 11 inches, for stirring ingredients in pint glasses or pitchers.
- **Microplane.** Fresh horseradish will thank you. The only way to extract aromatic and fresh horseradish is by microplace or blender, but I prefer grating with a microplane to order for each individual cocktail.
- **Jiggers.** Optional, but now that I've started working with jiggers, I trust and salute their consistency.

- **Bottle and can opener, or a church key.** For cans of tomato juice and beer backs.

- **Coasters or napkins.** This is a house party, right? Coasters are the soapboxes of the cocktail world. Let that cocktail stand on one and shout with pride. A coaster and even a napkin can also provide a little extra flair while preventing an icy glass from ruining your grandmother's end table.

6. Product. The word *product* is barspeak for booze. Since vodka is king in most Bloody Mary recipes, it's best to keep a couple of bottles handy (plan on 4 to 6 ounces for each guest), but there's nothing wrong with also sourcing bottles of gin and tequila, as well as something less common, such as aquavit, pisco, or mezcal (a smoky and delectable tequila alternative).

6a. Nonalcoholic product. Let's secure the necessities. When it comes to Bloody Marys, your vodka likes company, and what's good for the goose is good for the gander.

- **Tomato juice.** Please note that tomato juice can vary brand to brand and even from can to bottle. The good ones should be tasty enough to drink on their own. Tomato juice is full of nutritional value, offering antioxidants, potassium, iron, magnesium, niacin, thiamin, and vitamins A, B_6, C, and K. Some trusty brands are R.W. Knudsen, Campbell's, and Sacramento.

- **Clamato.** Clamato juice is primarily clam and tomato juice. As trailblazing bartenders would tell you, it's *really* tough to extract the juices from clams and tomatoes without the proper tools and machines we started using in the 1960s. So, there's no shame turning to the popular Clamato brand product.

- **Worcestershire sauce.** There's a good reason Lea and Perrins brand of Worcestershire sauce is on every bartender's shelf. Featuring a combination of tamarind, vinegar, molasses, lime, anchovy, onion, soy, and garlic, Worcestershire is responsible for elevating the Bloody Mary into stratospheric status.

- **Horseradish.** Gold's brand of prepared horseradish is completely reliable, but homemade, freshly grated horseradish cuts right to the heart and soul. Give it a shot. Fresh horseradish is the Harry Potter

It's the cocktail with a kick of spice, the world's best-loved hangover tonic, the only mixed drink unabashedly red, and the only one to sport, on occasion, a raffish celery stalk.

—JEFFREY M. POGASH, *BLOODY MARY*, 2011

wand–looking, possibly dirt-covered white carrot object in your grocery store. Wash and peel it, then grate a little over the top of your homemade Bloody. There's no substitute for the sharp, soul-awakening spice that comes from freshly grated horseradish. It has enhanced every Bloody it has ever met.

- **Salt.** Keep in mind that Worcestershire sauce and Clamato already have a hefty amount of sodium, so tread lightly with the salt. I recommend kosher salt, but if you use sea salt, keep in mind a little pinch goes a long way.

- **Pepper and a peppermill.** When using pepper, freshly ground is golden. Preground pepper loses its shelf life and flavor over time. A little known fact: pepper stimulates digestion. Another score for flavor!

- **Tabasco or other hot sauce.** The sky's the limit here: Frank's RedHot, Sriracha, Cholula, Crystal, and so on, will all work just fine.

- **Cayenne pepper.** It's not just for master cleanses anymore! Cayenne is the powdered aftermath of small dried red chile peppers that originate in French Guiana. Not only does it provide endorphins for brain activity, but it's also a decongestant. Cayenne's earthy, medium spice elevates the other ingredients working inside the Bloody parameters without pushing the heat into extreme territory.

- **Lemons and limes.** Not only are they terrific sources of vitamin C, but also the welcomed acidity from lemons and limes balances and brightens most beverages when properly applied. Both lemons and limes contribute sensational garnishes, from wheels, wedges, and peels to twists, tails, and flakes. Cut a lemon or lime in half and presto, you've created an ideal platform for rimming the lip of whatever glass you're now dipping in salt or spice for your Bloody. Lemons and tomatoes have been following each other since the beginning of tomato juice cocktails all the way through the Bloody Marys of today, and I would never make a michelada without fresh lime juice. If the Bloody is coming across as too spicy or sweet, the sour of citrus reestablishes balance.

- **Optional bonus materials.** Clam juice, beef broth, and various vegetable juices (carrot, beet, celery, and so on) will have the neighbors asking if they need to purchase tickets to your most talked-about party.

7. **Garnishes.** This list of is merely a jumping-off point. Think of the garnish bar the same way you would a build-your-own-sundae bar, where guests can revel in the assortment of goodies spread before their twinkling eyes. Necessary items include:

- **Celery.** Legend has it that the celery stalk first graced a Bloody Mary in the 1960s at Chicago's Pump Room, when a woman ordered a Bloody Mary that was served without the standard swizzle stick. She reached for the garnish tray and found a celery stalk, and thus revolutionized the future of garnishes.

- **Pickles or cornichons.** Sky's really the limit here. When it comes to pickled cucumbers, try dill, garlic, kosher dill, sweet/hot, or think beyond the cucumber by pickling other vegetables. See page 151 for an all-purpose vegetable brine so you can make your own DIY pickle bar.

- **Cocktail olives.** I prefer mine unstuffed and simply briny, as all olives should be, but Bloody Mary buffet bars near and far have implemented some impressive versions, from olives stuffed with blue cheese, pimento, anchovies, and even bacon!

- **Carrots.** Fresh carrots got nothing but crunch and texture for a Bloody.

- **Radishes.** Get that zinc! Fresh radishes give great bite to any Bloody.

- **Seasonings to rim the glass.** Cayenne, freshly ground black pepper, Old Bay, paprika, and the like are good options. To rim a glass, wet the lip of the glass with a piece of citrus fruit, ideally the lemon, lime, or orange you intend to use as a garnish. Dip the wet lip of the glass in the seasoning the way one salts a margarita, tapping off the excess. If you would like to rim half the glass in salt, apply citrus juice to the outside of one-half the rim—and be sure to not wet the inside of the glass, which will pick up more salt and inevitably fall inside your beverage.

8. **Personal Touches.** Leave no stone unturned when thinking about ingredients for a Bloody Mary. What's in your cupboard or refrigerator? Bring it out and see if it might work in a cocktail.

At our restaurants, the bar programs are at their best when we use the kitchen's ingredients. When we opened Fedora, we had barbecue potato chips on the menu. One day I walked into the kitchen, saw the barbecue

seasoning—cayenne, paprika, black pepper—and wondered, "Has anyone ever made barbecue syrup?" I took the three ingredients, boiled them down with sugar and water, and paired the syrup with bourbon, a spirit that complements those spices. The results made me happy, and our guests were thrilled to find a new cocktail on our menu the following week. Even if I had failed, I would've failed toward something interesting.

"rolling"

Most cocktails are stirred or shaken. Bloody Marys usually fall into the latter category. While I won't scoff at anyone who cares to shake their Bloody Mary—I recommend a simple five-second shake—I prefer the roll technique. The roll is a gentler method that slows the ice from melting. Shaking can dilute the flavors because the vigorous motion causes more ice to melt during and after the shake. When I'm drinking Bloodys, I'm want to taste all of the nuanced flavors that the spices, seasonings, and richness of tomato juice bring to the drink—not a bunch of melted ice!

how to roll

It's not rocket science. Just get a shaker with two tins, or two pint glasses, or any old two glasses that are large enough to contain your Bloody ingredients. Combine all of the ingredients in one glass or tin and fill with ice. Hold both tins (or glasses) a few inches apart from each another at chest level and pour the drink mixture between the vessels, trying to catch all of the liquid. Pour all of the ingredients back and forth from one vessel to the other three times. This, in essence, is "the roll." Again, you are free to shake your Bloody Marys, but please know that tomato juice is apt to fizz up when shaken, creating a foamier, effervescent beverage.

MFB* PROGRAM GARNISH OPTIONS

*Masters of Fine Bloodies

Beef straws, beef jerky, or cubes of filet mignon. Beef straws are nothing but wacky, pure meaty fun. Imagine a meat straw with a hole in the middle to sip on your Bloody. Now, imagine heaven. Benny's Original Meat Straws are available online.

Bacon

Cocktail onions

Soy sauce

Fresh herbs, such as mint, dill, fennel fronds, chive stalks

Poached, grilled, or barbecued shrimp

Boiled lobster tails

Watercress

Green onions

Boiled octopus tentacles

Hard-boiled eggs that have been pickled or flavored with soy

Pickled vegetables, such as green beans, beets, and fennel

Cucumber slices or wheels

Pickled caper berries

Honey

Endive

Caraway seeds

Fish sauce

Sliced avocado

Green, yellow, or red bell peppers

Fennel seeds

Sliced watermelon radish

Whole baby corn (canned)

Sliced jalapeño chiles

Oysters (just don't forget your shucking knife and safety glove)

Littleneck clams

Kimchee

Salmon, tuna, or avocado roll

Orange slices

Peeled, sliced ginger

Club soda (for sipping and for cleaning up spills!)

Beer

Bitters. Though only a few Bloody recipes call for bitters, having a bottle each of Angostura, Peychaud's, and orange bitters offers a well-balanced variety and works wonders for the guests who are only interested in drinking sparkling water.

what you can do ahead of the party

Premixing Bloody Marys is a terrific idea if for a party of ten or more, and it's absolutely necessary for groups of more than fifteen. If Bloodys are a featured cocktail, make it easier on you and your guests by prebatching the recipes in larger, sealable containers. To prebatch your Bloody Mary, mix together all of the ingredients *except* the alcohol and the ice. Some guests may want less alcohol in their beverage, so I suggest you add the alcohol as you make each drink. Try to prepare the Bloody Mary batches the day before and store them in the refrigerator. Allowing the mixture to sit overnight integrates the spices, seasonings, and tomato juice, elevating the umami flavor.

Incidentally, the Bloody Mary is one of the all-time best cocktails when it comes to using nonperishable garnishes. Olives, pickles, and pickled items have terrific shelf life and can often be refrigerated for up to a year after opening. Worcestershire, Tabasco, spices, and dried seasonings can last up to two years. Prepared horseradish can keep for three to four months.

Take an hour or so to prepare any fresh fruit, such as lemons, limes, and oranges, and any fresh herbs you might be using. Cutting citrus wedges ahead of time will also provide you with more opportunity to tell jokes or discuss who's going to win the big game. If you cut citrus a few hours before the party, it's perfectly fine left out at room temperature, but seal and refrigerate it if you want to use it the next day and discard any cut citrus after forty-eight hours. Citrus wheels and peels will dry out faster than wedges and should be cut and used within a few hours. Most fresh, uncut herbs can keep for approximately ten days in the refrigerator, but their color will definitely turn after four or five days.

I believe that if life gives you lemons, you should make lemonade . . . and try to find somebody whose life has given them vodka, and have a party.

—CALVIN TRILLIN

rules of the home cocktail game

If you are an untrained bartender, this small section is where I can assist you the most with hosting a cocktail party at home. I will help you "cut through the backyard," in my parlance. As a kid, you see, my best friends lived on the opposite corner of my block, so when I wanted to play with them, I often cut through my neighbors' backyards, much to their chagrin. But it got me to my friends faster!

1. Make sure you're dressed before the guests arrive (you never know when some early bird is going to show up). *One hour in advance.*

2. Set up the bar. Is there adequate surface area to prep and for guests to prep if they're building their own Bloodys? *One hour in advance.*

3. Set out all of the ingredients (mixers, garnishes, spirits), napkins, towels, trash cans, glassware, and barware (see "What You Can Do Ahead of the Party," page 36). *One to two hours in advance.*

4. Cue the music (this can be the first thing you do, as most non-music work can be counterproductive to readying one's party-hosting vibe). *I prefer music to be played first, the way LeBron prepares in the locker room before a big game.*

5. Are you sure you have enough ice? This should be one of the last ingredients you set out before guests start arriving, but it's also one of the most important, as melting ice on a hot summer day is no fun for anyone. *A comfortable time to ready the ice is within 30 minutes before t he party begins.*

6. Make water readily available for anyone smart enough to drink it. *Ready an hour or so before the party, and ongoing.*

7. Once guests start arriving, make sure the bar stays clean and well stocked. Your biggest test as a home bartender will be this maintenance. As Crash Davis says in *Bull Durham*, "When you win twenty in the show, *then* you can go back to having a messy bar, and the press will think you're colorful." *Ongoing.*

8. Refrain from arguing politics with any of your guests. *Ongoing.*

9. Refrain from controlling the karaoke machine. *Ongoing.*

10. Refrain from saying to a houseguest, "Let's have a drink in here" if "here" is the bedroom. *Ongoing.*

11. Probably not a good idea to fill any bathtubs with tomato juice, unless someone's been sprayed by a skunk. *Ongoing.*

12. Don't turn to your partner and say, "Let's go home and leave these nice people alone so they can clean up and get some sleep," only to have your partner say, "We *are* home, dummy." *End of party.*

There. Beautiful. You've succeeded as a home bartender if you've followed these rules.

guest rules

Hosts should not be the only ones to walk the plank of social etiquette. Guests need guidelines, too.

1. Don't drink straight from the liquor bottle.

2. Don't sing your high school fight song at the top of your lungs.

3. Your friend's sofa is not a hurdle and you are not trying to qualify for the Olympics.

4. Make sure the person you want to bear hug is *truly* okay with that sort of behavior before initiating.

5. No, the people you've only just met don't want to know how well you belch to "Give It Away" by the Red Hot Chili Peppers.

6. A thank-you travels for miles.

There. More beauty. More pizzazz. More soigné. Let the Bloody Mary party begin!

When people ask me if Dean Martin drank, let me put it this way: If Dracula bit Dean in the neck, he'd get a Bloody Mary.

—RED BUTTONS

Well, it's a Bloody
Mary morning
Baby left me without warning
Sometime in the night
So I'm flyin' down to Houston
Forgetting her's the nature
of my flight

—WILLIE NELSON, "BLOODY MARY MORNING"

PART 1

THE ORIGINALS

Every modern bartender, mixologist, and party host has his or her unique spin on the Bloody Mary. A modern-day Bloody pushes the boundaries of flavor, presentation, base spirit, even the vessel carrying it. People often muse on why the Bloody Mary is as popular as it is. Part of it certainly is that Bloody Marys are, like us, each a little different, each surprising and delightful in its uniqueness.

But before we go forward and celebrate all the weird and wonderful Bloody Marys out there, let's start with the classics. As the backyard lawn mower said to the garden tools, "Ease up, Lawn Team. Plenty of daylight to get wacky."

the "original" bloody mary

Old Mr. Boston's De Luxe Official Bartender's Guide, 1953
GARNISH none

Every great hero needs an origin story, right? Yet if you go hunting for the Bloody Mary creator you'll end up with limbs tucked into multiple rabbit holes. One thing is certain, though, and that is *when* this great drink came into the world. Around the end of Prohibition, not only did tomato juice become available, but also, crazy as it may sound, vodka became a thing. Pairing the two seems such an afterthought today, doesn't it?

To begin our fantastic voyage for the first Bloody Mary, let's keep it simple. This recipe celebrates the tomato juice cocktail and how vodka decided to crash the party.

SERVES 1

1½ OUNCES VODKA

1½ OUNCES TOMATO JUICE

1 DASH FRESHLY SQUEEZED LEMON JUICE

Combine all of the ingredients in an old-fashioned glass filled with ice. Stir until chilled and serve.

smirnoff brunch book bloody

DORIS MCFERRAN TOWNSEND, *The Smirnoff Brunch Book,* 1971
GARNISH celery stalk

By all rights, Smirnoff should have made it into a *Mad Men* storyline. Smirnoff's 1950s advertising campaigns brought America's undivided attention to the Bloody Mary. ("The Smirnoff Brunch: a time for coming together. *From the first twist of the Smirnoff cap, it's a party that simply happens. A party as easy as the eggs you scramble, as cheerful as the Bloody Marys you pour.*") Just as they did with vodka in the 1930s, Smirnoff's efforts snowballed and the Bloody Mary became a household name.

This Bloody subs A.1. steak sauce for Worcestershire. "Get involved!" as my friend Gabriel Stulman is wont to say when food is dropped in front of us.

SERVES 1

1½ OUNCES SMIRNOFF VODKA

3 OUNCES TOMATO JUICE

JUICE OF ½ LEMON

½ TEASPOON A.1. STEAK SAUCE

1 PINCH CELERY SALT

1 PINCH SALT

1 PINCH FRESHLY GROUND BLACK PEPPER

Combine all of the ingredients except the garnish in a cocktail shaker filled with ice. Roll the ingredients back and forth with another shaker 3 times, then strain and pour into an old-fashioned glass filled with ice. Garnish with a celery stalk.

gaz regan's bloody mary no. 2

GAZ REGAN, *The Bartender's Bible*, 1991
GARNISH slice of deseeded jalapeño chile

When Gary "gaz" Regan speaks about spirits, bartending, and life in general, I make a point to pay attention. It's no surprise gaz dedicated *The Bartender's Bible* to his mother, "who tolerates me living so far away from her," and to his wife, "who tolerates me living so near." It's important to always recognize the people responsible for making you a better person.

SERVES 1

4 OUNCES V8 JUICE

2 OUNCES CHILE-INFUSED VODKA (SEE NOTE)

Combine the V8 and vodka in a cocktail shaker filled with ice. Roll the ingredients back and forth with another shaker 3 times and strain into a highball glass filled with ice. Float the jalapeño slice on top.

Note: I quite like the Oola Distillery's chili pepper vodka from Seattle, Washington. Or you can make your own pepper-infused vodka: soak ½ cup crushed black peppercorns in a 750-milliliter bottle of at least 80-proof vodka for 24 hours; test every 6 to 8 hours for desired pepper spice.

old pepper

DAVID A. EMBURY, *The Fine Art of Mixing Drinks*, 1948
GARNISH none

David Embury wasn't even a bartender when he published his groundbreaking book in the late 1940s. Drinking was his hobby. When the world of bartending turned a corner in the early 2000s and got very serious about its origins, Mud Puddle Books resurrected Embury's cherished *Fine Art of Mixing Drinks*. I often return to its pages because it always reignites my inspiration.

This recipe is unique in that it swaps rye whiskey for vodka. Rye whiskey and all of its majestic spice brings a whole new perspective to the Bloody Mary. I like to use Ragtime Rye from New York Spirits, which has a 72 percent rye mash bill, for extra spice. Note that this recipe calls for chili sauce *or* tomato juice. I prefer chili sauce for added heat, but be sure to use a good old-fashioned chili sauce like the classic from Heinz. Avoid the sweeter stuff.

This recipe recommends using a sour glass, which is a smaller stemmed glass that holds 4 to 6 ounces. A short-stemmed wine glass or an old-fashioned glass works just fine.

SERVES 1

1½ OUNCES RYE WHISKEY

JUICE OF ½ LEMON

1 TEASPOON WORCESTERSHIRE SAUCE

1 TEASPOON CHILI SAUCE OR 1 TABLESPOON TOMATO JUICE

2 OR 3 DASHES ANGOSTURA BITTERS

1 DASH TABASCO SAUCE

Combine all of the ingredients in a cocktail shaker filled with ice. Roll the ingredients back and forth with another shaker 3 times and strain into a wine glass filled with ice.

smoked bloody bull

DALE DEGROFF, aka King Cocktail, *The Essential Cocktail,* 2008
GARNISH thick strip of orange zest

Dale DeGroff is profoundly connected to the history of the American cocktail. Though he's now known for being the founding member and president of the Museum of the American Cocktail, he was bartending in New York City at the famous Rainbow Room when most of us were still wandering aimlessly around in diapers in the 1980s. Contemporary bartenders with a passion for their craft will have a DeGroff recipe in their wheelhouse.

For anyone attempting to host a party, this recipe might win you some serious friend points, if not an afternoon of unbridled moxie. Dale DeGroff paved the way for the modern-day bartender, so thank you, King Cocktail, for your contributions near and far to the bartending world, thank you for the recipe, and most of all, thank you for your kindness.

SERVES 1

1½ OUNCES ABSOLUT VODKA

3 OUNCES BEEF BROTH (DALE PREFERS CAMPBELL'S)

2 OUNCES TOMATO JUICE

4 DASHES TABASCO SAUCE

1 DASH FRESHLY SQUEEZED ORANGE JUICE

1 PINCH FRESHLY GROUND BLACK PEPPER

Combine all of ingredients except the garnish in a shaker. Shake and strain into a cold-smoked goblet (see note) filled with ice. Garnish with an orange peel.

Note: The cold-smoked goblet is optional, but recommended. Either set the goblet in a tabletop smoker, or burn a small stick of hickory, applewood, cherry, mesquite, or walnut (careful, as walnut can overpower), then invert the glass over the smoldering wood for 30 seconds.

bullshot

DALE DEGROFF, aka King Cocktail, *The Essential Cocktail,* 2008
GARNISH 1 cooked strip of bacon, beef jerky, or if Dale
DeGroff is in the room, make it a thick strip of orange zest

Dale confessed to enjoying an even simpler version of the Bloody Bull,
the Bullshot, which cuts right through the nonsense. A Bullshot is
vodka, beef bouillon, perhaps some seasoning, perhaps some spice,
and that's it. However you decide to approach this fine beverage, drink
it quickly. After all, a shot is a shot.

SERVES 1

1½ OUNCES
ABSOLUT VODKA

4 OUNCES CHILLED
BEEF BOUILLON

2 DASHES
WORCESTERSHIRE SAUCE

1 PINCH SALT

1 PINCH FRESHLY
GROUND BLACK PEPPER

¼ TEASPOON HOT SAUCE
(OPTIONAL)

Combine all of the ingredients except the garnish in
a mixing glass filled with ice. Stir until chilled and
strain into a rocks glass filled with 1 to 3 ice cubes.
Garnish with bacon, beef jerky, or orange zest.

the red snapper

CROSBY GAIGE, *Crosby Gaige's Cocktail Guide and Ladies' Companion,* 1941
GARNISH lemon wedge

This recipe holds true to its conductor, Fernand "Pete" Petiot, and the King Cole Bar orchestra—a staff of seventeen bartenders—he started rehearsing and playing with in 1934. Noted epicurean Crosby Gaige published this recipe from the great St. Regis Hotel, a place that "maintains that touch of real home-life that forces the more conservative of fortune's favorites to forget their Lares and Penates and keeps them from sobbing in their sleep." Whoa.

This is the first printed Bloody Mary–esque recipe that includes cayenne and salt—the textbook seasonings we use today. The modern-day Bloody Mary owes a great deal to Mr. Petiot.

This recipe calls for a delmonico glass, which is a straight-sided 8- to 10-ounce cocktail glass. Substitute a highball or juice glass if you don't have one.

SERVES 1

2 OUNCES VODKA

2 OUNCES TOMATO JUICE

½ TEASPOON WORCESTERSHIRE SAUCE

1 DASH FRESHLY SQUEEZED LEMON JUICE

1 PINCH SALT

1 PINCH CAYENNE PEPPER

Combine all of the ingredients except the garnish in a cocktail shaker filled with ice. Roll the ingredients back and forth with another shaker 3 times and pour into a delmonico or highball glass. Serve with a lemon wedge.

I'm one of those passengers who arrives at the airport five or six hours early so I can throw back a few drinks and muster up the courage to board the plane. Apparently I'm not alone, because I've never been in an empty airport bar. I don't care what time you get there, even at 8 a.m. you have to fight your way to the bar. At that hour, everyone drinks Bloody Marys so no one can tell it's booze—at least until they fall off their chair.

—BOB NEWHART

mr. boston's bloody bloody mary

Old Mr. Boston's De Luxe Official Bartender's Guide, 1969
GARNISH sprig of mint

My mom has always ruled the kitchen, but my dad has one cupboard where he stows away his keys, papers, pipes, tobacco, and, always on the top shelf, his spirits.

My father's mint-condition 1969 *Old Mr. Boston's De Luxe Official Bartender's Guide* has been stationed in that hallowed cupboard since long before my first days on Earth. It's been used as a reference guide for impromptu cocktail tinkering and my parents always made it available to guests during dinner or card parties, as any good hosts would.

Powdered sugar was common in many cocktail recipes back in those days. This recipe also introduces celery salt to the playing field, which always elevates a flavor profile. The name Bloody Bloody Mary piques my curiosity: so nice they Bloodied it twice?

SERVES 1

1½ OUNCES OLD MR. BOSTON VODKA (OR, TO MODERNIZE, KETEL ONE)

3 OUNCES TOMATO JUICE

JUICE OF ½ LEMON

½ TEASPOON WORCESTERSHIRE SAUCE

¼ TEASPOON POWDERED SUGAR

1 INCH SALT

1 PINCH FRESHLY GROUND BLACK PEPPER

1 PINCH CELERY SALT

Combine all of the ingredients except the garnish in a cocktail shaker filled with ice. Roll the ingredients back and forth with another shaker 3 times and strain into an old-fashioned glass filled with ice. Garnish with a sprig of mint.

the stork club bloody mary

LUCIUS BEEBE, *Stork Club Bar Book,* 1946
GARNISH lemon wedge

This is the first published version of a Bloody Mary.

Bartenders and cocktail enthusiasts are explorers in the finest sense of the word. Each time we sip a new cocktail, spirit, or other ingredient, our minds run with thoughts on how the ingredients came into play. Among my favorite ways to respect the cocktails I make is to understand the history and lore behind them.

The more I researched early Bloody Mary recipes, the more I found variations of each ingredient—a great sign, in my opinion, as it reflects what exists in today's cocktail culture: endless experimentation.

This recipe calls for Angostura bitters, which are less hot than Tabasco but equally complex. Be wary of the amount of alcohol in this troublemaker.

SERVES 1

3 OUNCES VODKA

6 OUNCES TOMATO JUICE

2 DASHES ANGOSTURA BITTERS

JUICE OF ½ LEMON

Combine all of the ingredients except the garnish in a highball glass filled with ice. Stir until chilled and serve with a lemon wedge.

classic bloody caesar

WALTER CHELL, Westin Hotel, Calgary, Canada, 1969
GARNISH celery stalk and freshly shucked oyster on the half shell

In the late 1960s, Calgary Westin Hotel bar manager Walter Chell was asked to create something special. So he mashed up some clams, mixed their juice with tomato juice, and thus embraced the philosophy of "if it's good enough to eat, it's good enough to drink."

By the mid-1970s, the Bloody Caesar became Canada's most popular cocktail. Originally, making clam juice had been a sore spot for bartenders. Speaking as someone who would rather engage the guests than break my elbows mashing clams and tomatoes for hours, I salute the good people of Clamato with my healthy elbows, which are better used for high-fiving friends, strangers, and playful dogs. And so should every other bartender alive!

SERVES 1

1½ OUNCES VODKA

4 OUNCES CLAMATO JUICE

1 BARSPOON PREPARED HORSERADISH

2 DASHES WORCESTERSHIRE SAUCE

2 PINCHES FRESHLY GROUND BLACK PEPPER

1 PINCH CELERY SALT

1 PINCH SALT

Combine all of the ingredients except the garnish in a cocktail shaker filled with ice. Roll the ingredients back and forth with another shaker 3 times and strain into a rocks or highball glass filled with ice. Garnish with a celery stalk and serve with the oyster on the half shell atop the glass.

prairie oyster cocktail

OSCAR HAIMO, *Cocktail and Wine Digest,* 1948
GARNISH none

When Cocktail Kingdom's Greg Boehm introduced me to the published works of Oscar Haimo—the former president of the International Bar Managers' Association—I immediately saw his imprint on today's United States Bartenders' Guild and International Bartenders Association, two organizations that foster bartenders' professional development.

This recipe has everything: egg yolk, red pepper, Madeira, and even a dash of vinegar, which always makes me think of pickles and pickling. Some Madeiras have citrus and ginger notes, while others offer maple, walnut, and hints of beef bouillon. I can see any style of Madeira working for this recipe, but I enjoy Rare Wine Co.'s Savannah Madeira.

Oscar's recipe has been around since well before the craft cocktail train left the station. All aboard!

SERVES 1

1 EGG YOLK

1 DASH WORCESTERSHIRE SAUCE

⅛ TEASPOON RED PEPPER FLAKES

1 PINCH SALT

1½ OUNCES MADEIRA OR BRANDY

1 DASH DISTILLED WHITE VINEGAR

Place the egg yolk in an old-fashioned glass. Then pour the remaining ingredients except the vinegar into the glass, being careful not to break the egg yolk. Do not stir. No ice is needed. Top with the vinegar, then drink in one gulp, as if it were a shot. Grimace, wipe the dribble from your mouth, and get back to binge-watching *Game of Thrones.*

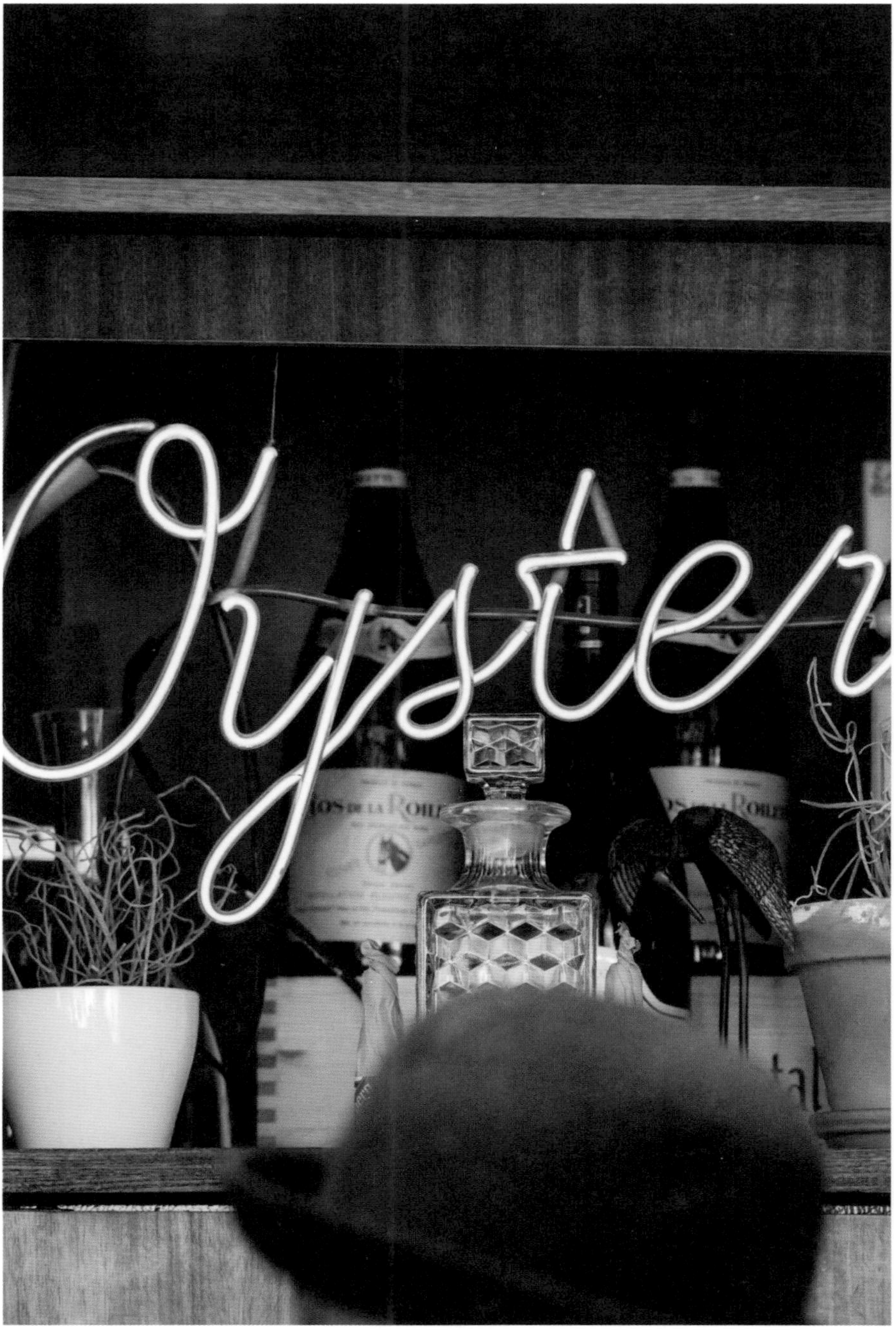
Oyster

trader vic's
bloody mary

Trader Vic's Book of Food and Drink, 1946
GARNISH lime wedge

Though Trader Vic was a tiki man until the end of time, including this early Bloody Mary recipe in the book about his world travels gives him mucho cool dude points. An adventurer, restaurateur, and prominent rum expert, Trader Vic wrote a book that will entertain anyone willing to read about—and believe—his adventures of seeing the far corners of our world.

Chilled tomato juice is key in making this bird sing. I would even go so far as to chill the bottle of vodka. Cold ingredients will save you from mixing the drink with ice and risking dilution.

SERVES 1

1½ OUNCES
CHILLED VODKA

1½ OUNCES CHILLED
TOMATO JUICE

Combine the vodka and tomato juice in an old-fashioned glass filled with ice. Stir until chilled and garnish with a lime wedge.

PART **2**

MODERN RECIPES

Willy Wonka: Invention, my dear friends, is 93 percent perspiration, 6 percent electricity, 4 percent evaporation, and 2 percent butterscotch ripple.

Mrs. Teevee: That's 105 percent!

Bloody Marys and creativity go hand in hand. Since everyone has a recipe, I felt it necessary to include some especially creative offerings from influential people in the cocktail and hospitality world. They're using a wide array of ingredients, and fresh juice or cold-pressed juice is, as the kids say, trending. And we all know what happens when the kids get ahold of something popular. I'm talking to you, MTV!

These imaginative recipes only scratch the surface of what's out there right now. My hope is that they inspire you to test new and exciting Bloody frontiers—or, at the very least, make you a shoo-in for Neighbor of the Year.

zuni café bloody

ZUNI CAFÉ, San Francisco, California
GARNISH celery stalk, lemon wedge, and a heaping
teaspoonful of Zuni Bar Salsa (see note)

Before I ever had a chance to visit San Francisco, I knew the heralded
Zuni Café would be a must-visit destination if I ever made my way west.
Once I got there, the triangular-shaped space gave me the feeling that
late chef-owner Judy Rodgers never took a day for granted. The wood-
fired cuisine and her spirit unfold with unequaled deftness. As a friend
stated, "Zuni has always made a sensational Bloody Mary; artisanal
before it was a byword."

SERVES 1

1½ OUNCES
SMIRNOFF VODKA

6 OUNCES TOMATO JUICE

¼ OUNCE AGED
BALSAMIC VINEGAR

2 DASHES TABASCO
SAUCE

2 GRINDS BLACK PEPPER

1 PINCH FINE SEA SALT

Combine all of the ingredients except the garnish in
a cocktail shaker filled with ice. Roll the ingredients
back and forth with another shaker 3 times and strain
into a pint glass filled with ice. Add the celery stalk
and stir once or twice. Garnish with a lemon wedge
and a spoonful of Zuni Bar Salsa.

Note: To make the Zuni Bar Salsa, simply combine
equal parts finely diced red onion and finely diced
red Fresno chile.

root down bloody mary

MIKE HENDERSON, Root Down, Denver, Colorado
GARNISH green onion, cornichon, cherry tomato, and pitted olive

Mike Henderson protected me every night we worked at Paul's Club in Madison, Wisconsin, as he bounced the front door while I bartended. When he decided to get behind the bar, I knew Mike was going places. All the way to Denver, in fact, where he now runs multiple beverage programs and protects the good people of Colorado with consistently creative and inspiring craft cocktails. Mike can school me in bartending up and down now—and still protect me from bullies on the playground.

The Root Down in the Denver International Airport goes through 35 to 40 gallons of this recipe in a week. Rev up the engines and vanish in a plume of Bloody good righteousness.

SERVES 1

1½ OUNCES VODKA OR GIN

6 OUNCES TOMATO JUICE

½ OUNCE DEMITRI'S CLASSIC BLOODY MARY SEASONING MIX OR OTHER SEASONING MIX

1 TABLESPOON FRESH CHOPPED DILL

1 TABLESPOON CHOLULA HOT SAUCE

1 TABLESPOON GOLD'S PREPARED HORSERADISH

Combine all of the ingredients except the garnish in a cocktail shaker filled with ice. Roll the ingredients back and forth with another shaker 3 times and strain into a pint glass filled with ice. Skewer the green onion, cornichon, cherry tomato, and olive on a cocktail pick and garnish.

sobelman's
bloody mary

DAVE SOBELMAN, Sobelman's Pub and Grill, Milwaukee, Wisconsin
GARNISH any or all of the cocktail skewers below (see note)

Sobelman's Pub and Grill has a condor's wingspan's worth of Bloody Mary options: the Standard, the Masterpiece (with a cheeseburger slider), the Baconado (with bacon-wrapped jalapeño cheese balls), the Bourbonado (skewered chicken wrapped in bacon and sweet bourbon sauce), the Crown Mary (topped with a Coronitas 7-ounce pony beer), and the Cheesehead (three 10-inch skewers of cheese). And then there's the one and only Beast, a bona fide 80-ounce mountain of Mary with all the fixings and a whole 3-pound fried chicken.

Sobelman's garnish game is stratospheric. Everything under the sun. Just make sure you use Wisconsin cheese for your garnish. "It's the only choice," says Dave Sobelman.

SERVES 1

2 OUNCES TITO'S VODKA

8 OUNCES JIMMY LUV'S BLOODY MARY MIX ("SHAKE THE BOTTLE, WAKE THE LUV!")

Combine the vodka and Bloody Mary mix in a cocktail shaker filled with ice. Roll the ingredients back and forth with another shaker 3 times and strain into a pint glass filled with ice. Dave notes that the garnish should stand up "like a floral arrangement."

Note: Get as crazy as you want with the options below.

Cocktail skewer No. 1: 1/3 pickled polish sausage and 1 cube Wisconsin Colby-Jack cheese

Cocktail skewer No. 2: 1 pickled Brussels sprout and 1 pickled onion

Cocktail skewer No.3: 1 dill pickle and 3 pitted olives

Cocktail skewer No. 4: 1 barbecued shrimp, 1 lemon wedge, and 1 grape tomato

Cocktail skewer No. 5: 1 pickled asparagus spear and 1 pickled scallion

commander's palace bloody

COMMANDER'S PALACE, New Orleans, Louisiana
GARNISH jalapeño pepper, pickled okra, sugarcane (optional), and freshly ground black pepper and coarse sea salt

New Orleans holds a special place in the heart of anyone who has ever visited. The people could not be more kind, thoughtful, and down to earth. It's more than just a party. It's a culture; an organism; a city so rich in history and depth there can only be one.

Commander's Palace's Bloody Mary keeps a firm grasp on the original recipe but does a terrific job of making it classic New Orleans. Each one is made with Creole seasoning and Crystal hot sauce, available at many of the neighborhood spots in and around the city, which is an important reminder: if the locals love it that much, say no more. At the restaurant, the garnishes are skewered on a piece of sugarcane, but at home, a cocktail pick will do just fine.

SERVES 1

CREOLE SEASONING, FOR THE RIM OF THE GLASS

1½ OUNCES VODKA

½ CUP V8 OR TOMATO JUICE

1 TEASPOON PREPARED HORSERADISH

1 TEASPOON OR 2 SPLASHES WORCESTERSHIRE SAUCE

4 DASHES CRYSTAL HOT SAUCE

2 DASHES TABASCO SAUCE

Coat the rim of a pint glass with Creole seasoning. Combine all of the remaining ingredients except the garnish in a cocktail shaker filled with ice. Roll the ingredients back and forth with another shaker 3 times, then strain into the rimmed glass filled with ice. Skewer the pepper, okra, and sugarcane on a cocktail pick and garnish.

If you like extra seasoning, top off the drink with a pinch of freshly ground pepper and coarse salt.

bunny mary

ROB KRUEGER, Extra Fancy, Brooklyn, New York
GARNISH large sprig of parsley and lemon wedge (optional)

I first had the chance to taste this almighty cocktail during an official Bloody Mary contest in New York (where even your shadow is happy to compete with you). In a field of around twenty-five different Bloodys, Rob's Bunny Mary took the prize. Not only is the name a winner, but also the drink's got orange-hued pizzazz in a field of red tulips.

SERVES 1

PIMENTÓN SALT, FOR THE RIM OF THE GLASS (PAGE 153)

1½ OUNCES VODKA OR AQUAVIT

3 OUNCES CARROT JUICE

½ OUNCE FRESHLY SQUEEZED LEMON JUICE

½ OUNCE HONEY SYRUP (EQUAL PARTS HONEY AND WATER)

1 TEASPOON CRYSTAL HOT SAUCE

1 TEASPOON CAPER BRINE

½ TEASPOON "4C" SALT (PAGE 153)

Coat the rim of a collins glass with the pimentón salt and fill with ice. Combine all of the remaining ingredients except the garnishes and stir until chilled. Garnish with a parsley sprig and a lemon wedge.

bill mary

BRIAN BARTELS, New York, New York
GARNISH slice of watermelon radish (optional)
and ice-cold bottle of Miller High Life (mandatory)

I wanted this drink to have some healing powers, as it's inspired by one of the more cathartic actors of all time: Bill Murray, whose great gift to the world is helping us laugh at the absurdity of it all. This healing tonic bridges coconut water-y goodness with a more traditional tomato profile.

Thank you, Bill Murray. Life is always a little easier with an extra laugh or two.

SERVES 1

SALT, FOR THE RIM OF
THE GLASS (OPTIONAL)

FRESHLY GROUND BLACK
PEPPER, FOR THE RIM OF
THE GLASS (OPTIONAL)

1½ OUNCES
SLOVENIA VODKA

1½ OUNCES
COCONUT WATER

1 OUNCE TOMATO WATER
(SEE RECIPE)

1 TEASPOON RED
PEPPER FLAKES

Coat half of the rim of a coupe or martini glass with salt, then coat the other half of the rim with pepper. Combine all of the remaining ingredients except the garnish in a shaker with ice. Shake vigorously for 10 seconds, or until the red pepper flakes release some heat. Strain into the glass and serve with a slice of watermelon radish and an ice-cold bottle of Miller High Life on the side. Cannonball comin'!

TOMATO WATER

MAKES 2 CUPS

10 HEIRLOOM OR BEEFSTEAK TOMATOES

Place the tomatoes in a bowl, cover, and freeze overnight. The following day, remove the tomatoes from the freezer to thaw. They will start to peel. Set up a fine-mesh sieve over another bowl. Once the tomatoes are completely thawed, peel them one at a time, and squeeze over the sieve and bowl to catch the liquid. The tomato water will keep for 3 days. Save the leftover tomato flesh for another use, such as sauce.

when the quinn cries mary

BRIAN BARTELS, Fedora, New York, New York
GARNISH pitted olive and lemon wedge

I have a friend named Quinn. I hope each and every one of you has a friend like him too. Quinn and I have known each other over twenty solid years. Quinn opened Fedora with us in 2011, and when he left, we decided to put a Quinn-named cocktail on every Fedora menu. Since his departure, we have served Dr. Quinn: Medicine Morman (as Quinn was raised Mormon, and, last I checked, was a man), Quinneth Paltrow, Quinnie the Pooh, Quinnside the Actors Studio, you get the picture.

This recipe combines Ancho Reyes ancho chile liqueur, a spicy-sweet Mexican bottling, and Hella Bitters smoked chili bitters. The base spirit is up to you; I prefer mezcal or Yaguara cachaça, as they elevate the Ancho Reyes.

SERVES 1

1 PINCH SALT

1 PINCH FRESH GROUND BLACK PEPPER

1 PINCH CELERY SALT

¾ OUNCE MEZCAL, CACHAÇA, OR VODKA

¾ OUNCE ANCHO REYES ANCHO CHILE LIQUEUR

2½ OUNCES TOMATO JUICE

¼ OUNCE SOY SAUCE

4 DASHES HELLA BITTERS SMOKED CHILI BITTERS

Mix the salt, pepper, and celery salt together on a small plate. Coat half of the rim of a rocks glass with the salt mixture. Combine the mezcal, Ancho Reyes, tomato juice, and soy sauce in a cocktail shaker filled with ice. Roll the ingredients back and forth with another shaker 3 times. Fill the rimmed glass with ice and strain the cocktail into it. Top with the bitters and garnish with an olive and a lemon wedge.

la boîte bloody mary

JIM MEEHAN, PDT, New York, New York
GARNISH celery stalk

Bloody Marys were a big deal at Paul's Club, the unforgettable bar in Madison, Wisconsin, where Jim and I worked in college. True tradition: Jim won't shake my hand, opting instead for the Arsenio Hall finger touch and roll. Like any characteristic of an extraordinary friend, it always brings a smile to my face.

Years later, Jim cultivated a Bloody Mary Spice Series with the La Boîte brand of specialty spices, with each spice mix meant to accompany a specific spirit. It's safe to say they're all worth sampling, as I don't know any other bartender passionate enough to work with a spice specialist on what makes the nuances of flavor so complex yet so balanced and approachable. As Chuck D says, hear the drummer get wicked!

SERVES 1

1½ OUNCES VODKA

4 OUNCES TOMATO JUICE

¼ OUNCE FRESHLY SQUEEZED LEMON JUICE

¼ OUNCE FRESHLY SQUEEZED LIME JUICE

¼ OUNCE LEA AND PERRINS WORCESTERSHIRE SAUCE

½ TEASPOON GOLD'S PREPARED HORSERADISH

½ TEASPOON LA BOÎTE B-MARY SPICE BLEND (SEE NOTE)

¼ TEASPOON CHOLULA HOT SAUCE

Combine all of the ingredients in a cocktail shaker filled with ice. Roll the ingredients back and forth with another shaker 3 times. Fine-strain into a pint glass filled with ice. Garnish with a celery stalk.

Note: You can substitute a mixture of smoked paprika, celery seeds, black pepper, Szechuan, cayenne, and salt if you can't find the La Boîte blend.

la boîte bloody maria

JIM MEEHAN, PDT, New York, New York
GARNISH pickled tomatillo (see page 151),
pickled whole jalapeño, or lime wedge

A Bloody Mary with tequila is called a Bloody Maria. *Sí, siempre.* Grapefruit brightens the earthy, pepper-nuanced qualities of tequila in this south-of-the-border spin on a classic Bloody Mary. A pickled jalapeño or wedge of lime would work nicely in place of the tomatillos.

SERVES 1

4 OUNCES TOMATO JUICE

1½ OUNCES
BLANCO TEQUILA

¼ OUNCE
WORCESTERSHIRE SAUCE

¼ OUNCE FRESHLY
SQUEEZED LIME JUICE

¼ OUNCE
FRESHLY SQUEEZED
GRAPEFRUIT JUICE

½ TEASPOON LA BOÎTE
B-MARIA SPICE BLEND
(SEE NOTE)

½ TEASPOON GOLD'S
PREPARED HORSERADISH

½ TEASPOON TABASCO
CHIPOTLE SAUCE

Combine all of the ingredients except the garnish in a cocktail shaker filled with ice. Roll the ingredients back and forth with another shaker 3 times. Double-strain into a collins glass filled with ice. Garnish with a pickled tomatillo, pickled whole jalapeño, or lime wedge.

Note: You can substitute a mixture of dried green chile, cilantro, and chipotle if you can't find the La Boîte blend.

mary on holiday (virgin mary)

BRIAN BARTELS, New York, New York
GARNISH surfboard-shaped slice of cucumber (see note), lemon wheel, slice of heirloom tomato, and sprig of mint

I came up with this drink one evening toward the end of summer, when temperatures can unexpectedly drop overnight. Not only does that catch us off guard, but also we can catch a cold! So what better way to boost our immune systems than with juice—and the occasional break from liquor. Did I just say that? For the ginger beer, I prefer Fever-Tree—it's extra-spicy and feels vaguely healthy.

If you must make an alcoholic version, add something peppery for your spirit selection. I salute Oola chili pepper vodka, Absolut Peppar vodka, and Stoli Hot jalapeño vodka.

SERVES 1

2 OUNCES GINGER BEER

1½ OUNCES PINEAPPLE JUICE

1½ OUNCES TOMATO JUICE

¾ OUNCE FRESHLY SQUEEZED LEMON JUICE

½ OUNCE HONEY SYRUP (EQUAL PARTS HONEY AND WATER)

2 PINCHES CAYENNE PEPPER

Combine all of the ingredients except the garnish in a cocktail shaker filled with ice. Roll the ingredients back and forth with another shaker 3 times and strain into a highball glass filled with ice. Garnish with slices of cucumber and tomato, a lemon wedge, and a mint sprig.

Note: Make your friends jealous by posting this drink on Instagram with a cucumber cut in the shape of a surfboard. Just cut a lengthwise slice of cucumber so that it's ⅛ inch thick, preferably with a mandoline. And with the additional slice of heirloom tomato, lemon wheel, and/or mint sprig, this healthy drink goes to eleven. Huzzah!

the great dane michelada

BRIAN BARTELS, New York, New York
GARNISH dill pickle

Bartending is a gateway for some people, but for me, it's about hosting a party, helping people, and seeking something meaningful about humanity in ways we cannot always articulate. So when I got the chance to learn how to be a bartender at the Great Dane, my life changed. Though they don't serve this cocktail at the Great Dane, I wanted to create one on their behalf. It's because of the Great Dane that you're getting the chance to read this book, as the first cocktail I ever learned to make was the Bloody Mary (for an avalanche of Wisconsin drinkers and brunch attendees). #Daner4Life.

If you prefer no ice, use a highball glass instead of the pint glass.

SERVES 1

DANER 4LIFE CHILI SALT, FOR THE RIM OF THE GLASS (PAGE 153)

1 OUNCE AQUAVIT

1 OUNCE TOMATO JUICE

½ OUNCE FRESHLY SQUEEZED ORANGE JUICE

½ OUNCE FRESHLY SQUEEZED LIME JUICE

½ OUNCE CHOLULA HOT SAUCE

½ TEASPOON LA BOÎTE B-MARION MIX (SEE NOTE)

4 DASHES WORCESTERSHIRE SAUCE

CRISP, LIGHT LAGER, FOR TOPPING OFF

Coat half of the rim of a pint glass with chili salt. Combine all of the remaining ingredients except the lager and garnish in a cocktail shaker filled with ice. Roll the ingredients back and forth with another shaker 3 times. Fill the rimmed glass with ice and strain the cocktail into it. Top off with the lager, garnish with a pickle, and serve.

Note: If you don't have the La Boîte Marion spice mix handy, an acceptable substitute is a pinch of each cayenne, ground anise, ground caraway, and ground black pepper.

cucumber snapper

BRIAN BARTELS, Fedora, New York, New York
GARNISH lemon wheel

Growing up, I never had a taste for cucumbers. Boy, am I glad I grew up! The more I surround myself with them, the more cucumbers seem to go with just about everything, especially Bloodys.

This recipe doesn't have much in the way of heat and spice, and that's the point. One could say this celebrates the vegetal complexity of its components, offering a refreshing, citrusy waterfall of flavor. Tomatoes, cucumber, and ginger to show, and taste buds for the win!

SERVES 1

DILL SALT, FOR THE RIM
OF THE GLASS (PAGE 154)

1½ OUNCES
HENDRICK'S GIN

1 OUNCE FRESH
CUCUMBER JUICE
(SEE NOTE)

1 OUNCE
TOMATO JUICE

1 OUNCE FEVER-TREE
GINGER BEER

3 DASHES HELLA BITTERS
GINGER LEMON BITTERS

Coat the rim of an old-fashioned glass with dill salt. Combine all of the remaining ingredients except the garnish in a cocktail shaker filled with ice. Roll the ingredients back and forth with another shaker 3 times. Fill the rimmed glass with ice and strain the cocktail into it. Garnish with a lemon wheel.

Note: To make the cucumber juice, use either a juicer or puree the cumber in a high-powered blender and then strain through a fine-mesh sieve.

pb&j & mary

BRIAN BARTELS, New York, New York
GARNISH crushed Seasoned Peanuts (recipe follows),
peanut butter–dipped celery stalk, and 3 or 4 turns
of freshly ground black pepper

This cocktail was created for Harry Dean Stanton, quiet king of the silver
screen. Not because he's known for any roles where he eats peanuts
or peanut butter; just because if I had a little extra peanut butter, I
would be obliged to share it with Harry Dean. Kris Kristofferson once
wrote music lyrics about Harry Dean, proclaiming, "He's a walking
contradiction, partly truth and party fiction."

Feel free to substitute Herradura reposado tequila, which has a
peanutty profile, for the vodka, or any jam you'd like for the strawberry
(I prefer strawberry, as I am still eight years old). The peanut infusion
time depends solely on how nutty you want it to be. Good things come
to those who wait, all you undiscovered movie stars.

SERVES 1

1½ OUNCES PEANUT-
INFUSED VODKA OR
TEQUILA (PAGE 154)

4 OUNCES TOMATO JUICE

1½ TABLESPOONS
STRAWBERRY JAM

¾ OUNCE CHOLULA
HOT SAUCE

½ OUNCE FRESHLY
SQUEEZED LEMON JUICE

½ TEASPOON
WORCESTERSHIRE SAUCE

Combine all of the ingredients except the garnish in a
cocktail shaker filled with ice. Shake until the fruit jam
is fully combined. Strain into an old-fashioned glass
filled with ice. Garnish with the seasoned peanuts,
peanut butter–dipped celery stick, and pepper. Best
to keep the peanut butter end of the celery stick
outside of the liquid.

SEASONED PEANUTS
MAKES 1 CUP

1 TABLESPOON
CAYENNE PEPPER

1 CUP DRY-ROASTED PEANUTS

1 TABLESPOON PAPRIKA

Preheat the oven to 200°F. Mix the cayenne and paprika
in a small bowl, then toss with the peanuts. Transfer to
a baking sheet and roast for 12 to 15 minutes. Let cool.
Store in an airtight container for up to 1 week.

irish goodbye mary

BRIAN BARTELS, New York, New York
GARNISH boiled Yukon gold or fingerling potato, carrot, and/or celery stalk

I love a good Irish goodbye, when someone who has been attending a special gathering—often involving alcohol—pulls the classic move of waiting until everyone's distracted by sports, fireworks, or a naked leprechaun, then sneaks out the bar's back door!

Be mindful–there's no pot of tomato juice at the end of this rainbow, which is where the beet juice comes into play. Beet juice can be bought prebottled in most supermarkets, but if you're having a hard time tracking it down, tomato juice will save the day.

SERVES 1

2 ½ OUNCES GUINNESS STOUT OR OTHER CREAMY, COFFEE-CHOCOLATE STOUT

1 OUNCE JAMESON IRISH WHISKEY

2 OUNCES BEET JUICE

1 OUNCE BEEF BROTH

1 GENEROUS PINCH SALT

2 GENEROUS PINCHES FRESHLY GROUND BLACK PEPPER

1 DASH SPICY BITTERS (OPTIONAL)

Combine all of the ingredients except the garnish in a mixing glass filled with ice. Stir and strain into a pint glass filled with ice. Garnish with the potato, carrot, and/or celery stalk.

january 1 cocktail

BRIAN BARTELS, New York, New York
GARNISH lemon wedge

Is it any surprise that New Year's Day is National Bloody Mary Day?

Many people feel awkward and socially challenged the day after the most awkward and socially challenging night of the year, when for a few painfully magical hours, we all get to live as one of the main characters in a John Hughes film. New Year's Eve is a beast we hope to tame, but rarely do. And the next day we're doomed to suffer the posttraumatic physical malady known as the hangover. Many words have been used to describe this feeling. Is "ouch" a feeling? That's what I would call it. Or ugh. Is "ugh" a feeling? What about "me-owwwwww"?

When it comes to the vodka here, pick something high quality, like Absolut Elyx or St. George Green Chile—you deserve the good stuff on New Year's Day. And here's the best news: you're welcome to have another since you liked the first so much.

SERVES 1

1 OUNCE HIGH-QUALITY VODKA

2 OUNCES TOMATO JUICE

4 DASHES WORCESTERSHIRE SAUCE

4 DASHES EL YUCATECO GREEN HABANERO HOT SAUCE (OR GREEN TABASCO)

2 PINCHES SALT

3 TURNS FRESHLY GROUND BLACK PEPPER

Combine all of the ingredients except the salt, pepper, and garnish in an old-fashioned glass with ice. Stir until chilled. Don't bother with a salted rim. Drop the salt and black pepper over the top. Garnish with a lemon wedge.

umami mary

KENTA GOTO, Bar Goto, New York, New York
GARNISH pitted olive

Kenta developed quite a following while bartending at Audrey Saunders's terrific Pegu Club cocktail bar. He brought the necessary balance of creativity and attention to every drinker he served, and his humble craftsmanship knows no limits. Bar Goto opened after Kenta worked with us at Bar Sardine, and the Umami Mary—which has been on Bar Goto's menu since day one—spins the classic recipe by substituting miso for Worcestershire, a playful and savory win.

SERVES 1

1 ¾ OUNCES SHIITAKE-INFUSED VODKA (PAGE 156)

2 OUNCES TOMATO JUICE

2 OUNCES CLAMATO JUICE

¾ OUNCE FRESHLY SQUEEZED LEMON JUICE

¼ TEASPOON WHITE MISO

1 PINCH GROUND RED CHILE (OPTIONAL)

Combine all of the ingredients except the garnish in a bowl and whisk until the miso dissolves thoroughly. Pour the ingredients over ice into a highball glass and gently stir until chilled. Skewer the olive on a cocktail stick and garnish.

parker compound bloody mary

SAM PARKER, the Parker Compound, Madison, Wisconsin
GARNISH snit of Pacifico or Carta Blanca beer (see note) and celery salt

Sam Parker first taught me how to bartend, so I owe him, well, my life. But apart from that, I don't charge him to tell anyone I'm his good friend, so even steven. Sam and his wife Betsy host the best meals out of their home, affectionately called the Parker Compound. As such, this recipe could easily fit into the "Hosting a Party" chapter, but it's included in the "Modern Recipes" chapter, which can be dubbed "original," as there are few who are more original than Sam Parker. Sam's ruling: Smirnoff is fine. ("You don't have to waste the good stuff on a Bloody, but this does not mean Siberian Ice is acceptable. Have some class. Only use Sacramento brand tomato juice. Try not to have nine.")

SERVES 1

2 OUNCES SMIRNOFF VODKA

1 OUNCE SACRAMENTO TOMATO JUICE

JUICE OF ½ LEMON

4 DASHES TABASCO SAUCE

2 DASHES WORCESTERSHIRE SAUCE

Combine all of the ingredients except the garnishes in a cocktail shaker filled with ice. Roll the ingredients back and forth with another shaker 3 times and strain into a pint or double rocks glass filled with ice. Top off with some beer from your snit and garnish with a pinch of celery salt.

Note: A *snit* is a Midwestern term for a beer back, or back, which many of us enjoy with our Bloody Marys. Also known as shorty, chaser, nip, tot, or, my favorite, pony. The biggest difference among these terms is in the volume. A snit is the equivalent of 2 jiggers, or 3 ounces. The other terms will get you different measurements or perhaps just weird looks from your Midwestern bartender, who will probably tilt his head and contemplate what to watch on Netflix after his shift.

aylesbury bloody mary

SIMON FORD, partner and brand ambassador, The 86 Co.
GARNISH lemon wedge, lime wedge, and celery stalk

This is probably the modern recipe that's closest to the original, which is fitting for noble everyman Simon Ford. He enters and leaves every room like a proper bartender: with a smile on his face. Simon has solidified himself in the modern echelon of bartending, craft cocktails, and the next frontier of spirits. Tallyho! Onward and upward, spirit soldiers.

Simon says: "My favorite way to make a Bloody Mary is rather simple . . . It's quite similar to the classic, but I love to float dry sherry—and fresh citrus is key."

SERVES 1

SALT, FOR THE
RIM OF THE GLASS

FRESHLY GROUND BLACK
PEPPER, FOR THE RIM OF
THE GLASS

1½ OUNCES AYLESBURY
DUCK VODKA

3 OUNCES TOMATO JUICE

½ OUNCE FRESHLY
SQUEEZED LEMON JUICE

4 DASHES
TABASCO SAUCE

2 DASHES
WORCESTERSHIRE SAUCE

SPLASH OF FINO SHERRY

Mix the salt and pepper together on a small plate. Coat half of the rim of a highball glass with the salt and pepper mixture. Combine the vodka, tomato juice, lemon juice, Tabasco, Worcestershire, a pinch of salt, and a pinch of pepper in a cocktail shaker filled with ice. Roll the ingredients back and forth with another shaker 3 times. Fill the rimmed glass with ice and strain the cocktail into it. Float the sherry on top and garnish with a lemon wedge, a lime wedge, and a celery stalk.

bloody ramen

MATT GRIFFIN, Bar Sardine, New York, New York
GARNISH ½ soy egg, charred shishito pepper, and charred green onion (see notes)

Chef Matt Griffin is one of the most hardworking people I know. He lives, breathes, sleeps, and eats inspiration. Outside of quoting great lines from *A River Runs Through It*, Matt holds a steadfast passion for ramen. When we opened Bar Sardine, we wanted a cocktail category devoted to Bloody Mary variations. With ramen on his mind, Matt came up with this gem. The soy and ramen beef broth offer a savory spin on a Bullshot (page 52), with the hearty, bona fide tomatoey richness balancing the spice. You can shoot the shoots with the best of them, Chef Matt.

SERVES 1

TOGARASHI, FOR THE RIM OF THE GLASS

2 OUNCES REYKA VODKA

3 OUNCES BEEF BOUILLON BROTH

1½ OUNCES TOMATO JUICE

¾ OUNCE FRESHLY SQUEEZED LIME JUICE

BEER CHASER

Coat the rim of a cider glass with togarashi. Combine all of the remaining ingredients except the beer and garnish in a cocktail shaker filled with ice. Roll the ingredients back and forth with another shaker 3 times. Fill the rimmed glass with ice and strain the cocktail into it. Garnish with a soy egg, charred green onion, and shishito pepper. Complete the circle with a dry, crisp lager served on the side.

Notes: To make a soy egg, peel the shell from a hard-boiled egg and submerge in soy sauce for 4 hours. Store in a sealed container and refrigerate for up to 5 days. When ready to use, cut the egg in half lengthwise.

To char the green onion and shishito pepper, toss them with a little olive oil and salt, then grill over medium heat, turning often, until charred, approximately 2 minutes. Let cool and serve.

PART **3**

HOSTING A PARTY

I truly believe the Bloody Mary is about nostalgia. It's a remembrance of things past (be they stored in sobriety or aided by libations) and how we arrive between moments. Hosting parties with friends offers us the opportunity to share in these stories. When friends or colleagues host an event out of their own home, we get an opportunity to visit and share the day-to-day with others. There's something remarkably celebratory about that, as I don't think it's an easy task to hope guests enjoy themselves while said host bounces all over the rooms in constant update mode. So remember to always thank your hosts. Especially if they're attempting one of these recipes for a large group of people— and certainly if they're still "feeling it" from the night before.

a note on yields

Please note that most of the recipes in this section reflect the best of both worlds—ratios for a single serving accompanied by a batch for ten people. You'll get better and more consistent Bloodys if you make each one to order, but if time is of the essence, you can mix all the ingredients together in a pitcher with a 2-quart capacity. Then you can make it easy on yourself and focus on all the other party accessories you still need to solidify, like your unbeatable homemade guacamole, spicy chocolate popcorn, and red pepper–peanut butter hummus. Hey, where's my invitation?!

the publican
bloody mary

TERRY ALEXANDER, partner, and **MICHAEL RUBEL,**
bartender, The Publican, Chicago, Illinois
GARNISH lemon wedge, garlic dill pickle spear,
and your choice of pickled vegetable (optional)

Here's a mix recipe for two, the cocktail equivalent of walking into a
fancy hotel lobby with that special someone, and instead of heading
up to your room, taking a seat on their little loveseat for two. From
there, you soak in all the comers and goers, just chatting, unwinding.
No need to be anywhere else. Romantically inert. Is this a cocktail
book or a sequel to *Before Sunset*? My guess is The Publican has many
love stories from people bonding over their celebrated Bloody Mary.

SERVES 1

2 OUNCES MODEST
VODKA

7 OUNCES PUBLICAN
BLOODY MIX (SEE RECIPE)

Combine the vodka and Bloody mix in a cocktail
shaker filled with ice. Roll the ingredients back and
forth with another shaker 3 times and strain into a
pint glass filled with ice. Garnish with a lemon wedge,
garlic dill pickle spear, and pickled vegetable.

PUBLICAN BLOODY MIX
SERVES 2, WITH SOME EXTRA FOR TOPPING OFF
(LOVESEAT NOT INCLUDED)

15 OUNCES TOMATO JUICE

½ OUNCE WORCESTERSHIRE
SAUCE

¼ OUNCE FRESHLY
SQUEEZED LEMON JUICE

1 ANCHOVY

½ TEASPOON CHINESE
HOT MUSTARD

½ TEASPOON SALT

½ TEASPOON FRESHLY
GROUND BLACK PEPPER

½ TEASPOON CELERY SALT

½ TEASPOON SRIRACHA
SAUCE

Combine all of the ingredients in a blender and
blend until smooth. Store in a sealed container
and refrigerate for up to 1 week.

green bay bloody mary

BRIAN BARTELS, Bar Sardine, New York, New York
GARNISH cornichon, lengthwise slice of cucumber, and celery stalk

When we opened Bar Sardine in the summer of 2014, we wanted an all-day Bloody Mary on the menu, and call me Dr. Seuss, but I couldn't stop thinking about green green green Bloodys.

Tomatillos can be a little fussy with size and consistency, and in the winter, they tend to grow sour after sitting for a day or two. But when they behave, wow. High-five somebody.

SERVES 1

CELERY SALT, FOR THE
RIM OF THE GLASS

1½ OUNCES DEATH'S
DOOR VODKA
(ON, WISCONSIN!)

4 OUNCES GREEN BAY
BLOODY BLEND
(SEE RECIPE)

½ OUNCE FRESHLY
SQUEEZED LEMON JUICE

3 DASHES
WORCESTERSHIRE
SAUCE

Coat half of the rim of a cider or pint glass with celery salt. Combine all of the remaining ingredients except the garnish in a cocktail shaker filled with ice. Roll the ingredients back and forth with another shaker 3 times. Fill the half-rimmed cider glass with ice and strain the cocktail into the glass. Garnish with a cornichon and a lengthwise cucumber slice wrapped around the inside of the glass or rolled into the celery stalk.

GREEN BAY BLOODY BLEND
MAKES 40 OUNCES, ENOUGH FOR 10 DRINKS

1¼ POUNDS CUCUMBER
(APPROXIMATELY 1¼
CUCUMBERS)

10 OUNCES TOMATILLOS
(6 TO 8 TOMATILLOS)

10 FRESH PARSLEY LEAVES

¾ TEASPOON FRESHLY
GROUND BLACK PEPPER

¾ TEASPOON CELERY SALT

¾ TEASPOON SALT

1½ OUNCES GREEN
TABASCO SAUCE

In a blender, blend all of the ingredients on low speed until the mixture turns smooth.

Seal in a nonreactive container and keep refrigerated for up to 1 week.

sardine bloody

NATE KINDERMAN, Sardine, Madison, Wisconsin
GARNISH lime wedge; lemon wedge; a skewer with 2 pitted
olives, a cornichon, a slice of jalapeño, and a radish; and a
beer chaser

For those of you who have never traveled to Wisconsin, I leave you with the words of John Steinbeck in *Travels with Charley (In Search of America)*:

"To awaken here might make one believe it is a dream of some other planet, for it has a non-earthly quality, or else the engraved record of a time when the world was much younger and much different."

Wisconsinites are nothing if not hardworking, polite, good-natured folk, often inclined to say hello to a stranger, hold doors open for everyone, and remain perpetually grateful for what they've been given in life. This Bloody, with floral notes and balanced spice, and accompanied by a beer chaser, is a terrific example of Wisconsin's heritage.

SERVES 1

CELERY SALT, FOR THE
RIM OF THE GLASS

2 OUNCES SVEDKA
VODKA OR BEET-INFUSED
VODKA (PAGE 155)

6 OUNCES SARDINE
BLOODY MIX (PAGE 101)

4 OUNCES
KRONENBOURG 1664

Coat the rim of a pint glass with celery salt. Combine the vodka and Bloody mix in a cocktail shaker filled with ice. Roll the ingredients back and forth with another shaker 3 times. Fill the rimmed glass with ice and pour the cocktail into it, then garnish with a lime wedge and the skewered vegetables. Because Sardine is in Wisconsin, each Bloody is served with a Kronenbourg 1664 beer chaser.

SARDINE BLOODY MIX

MAKES 2 QUARTS, ENOUGH FOR 10 DRINKS

1 GENEROUS TEASPOON CHOPPED GARLIC

2 OUNCES PERNOD PASTIS

3½ OUNCES WORCESTERSHIRE SAUCE

¼ OUNCE TABASCO SAUCE

2 TABLESPOONS CELERY SALT

2 HEAPING TEASPOONS FRESHLY GROUND BLACK PEPPER

¼ CUP PREPARED HORSERADISH

½ CUP FRESHLY SQUEEZED LEMON JUICE

½ CUP FRESHLY SQUEEZED LIME JUICE

38 OUNCES V8 JUICE

Combine all of the ingredients in a large container and stir until combined. Transfer to a pitcher if serving immediately, or store in a sealed container and refrigerate for up to 7 days.

shannon's sangrita/ michelada

SHANNON PONCHE, Leyenda and Clover Club, Brooklyn, New York
GARNISH lime wedge

Sangritas ("little blood" in Spanish) were created as terrific sipping accompaniments to tequila. Here, the wildly talented part-ninja Shannon Ponche pairs them with micheladas in a crafty combo of juices and spices. People pay a lot of money to see art in museums, so I would recommend sitting at Shannon's bar some day to witness art in motion, all for the low, low price of a delicious drink.

SERVES 1

SALT, FOR THE
RIM OF THE GLASS

2 OUNCES CARROT-
PAPAYA SANGRITA
(SEE RECIPE)

½ OUNCE FRESHLY
SQUEEZED LIME JUICE

NEGRA MODELO BEER

Coat half of the rim of a chilled pint glass with salt. Combine the sangrita and lime juice in the rimmed glass, then top off with the beer and garnish with a lime wedge. It also doesn't hurt to crack open the cold beer while preparing the sangrita, as life, not unlike the fireworks on the Fourth of July, can be far too short.

CARROT-PAPAYA SANGRITA
MAKES 2½ CUPS, ENOUGH FOR 10 DRINKS

9 OUNCES PERFECT PURÉE
PAPAYA PUREE

9 OUNCES CARROT JUICE

1¼ OUNCES FRESHLY
SQUEEZED LIME JUICE

1¼ OUNCES FRESHLY
SQUEEZED ORANGE JUICE

1 TEASPOON GROUND
GUAJILLO CHILE POWDER

½ TEASPOON GROUND
CHIPOTLE CHILE POWDER

¾ TEASPOON SALT

Combine all of the ingredients and let sit for 1 hour. Pass through a fine-mesh strainer lined with cheesecloth or a coffee filter. Transfer to a pitcher if serving immediately, or store in a sealed container and refrigerate for up to 2 days.

the covina bloody mary

TED KILPATRICK, Covina, New York, New York
GARNISH cocktail onion, pitted olive, and pepperoncini

This little number wields a terrific balance. Freshly prepared horseradish helps make this unique. The level of concentrated flavor to spice is unparalleled. Have two!

SERVES 1
2 OUNCES TITO'S VODKA
5½ OUNCES COVINA BLOODY MARY MIX (SEE RECIPE)

Combine the vodka and Bloody mix in a cocktail shaker filled with ice. Roll the ingredients back and forth with another shaker 3 times and strain into a pint glass filled with ice. Skewer your choice of 2 of the garnishes on a cocktail pick and garnish.

COVINA BLOODY MARY MIX
MAKES 2 QUARTS, ENOUGH FOR 10 DRINKS

1 (46-OUNCE) BOTTLE SACRAMENTO TOMATO JUICE

5 OUNCES FRESHLY SQUEEZED LEMON JUICE

5 OUNCES WORCESTERSHIRE SAUCE

3 TABLESPOONS FRESHLY PREPARED HORSERADISH (SEE NOTE)

2½ OUNCES SOY SAUCE

2½ OUNCES CHOLULA HOT SAUCE

2 TEASPOONS OLD BAY SEASONING

1 TEASPOON CELERY SALT

1 TEASPOON FRESHLY GROUND BLACK PEPPER

Combine all of the ingredients in a large pitcher. Store in a sealed container and refrigerate at least overnight, to allow the flavors to integrate, and up to 7 days.

Note: To make freshly prepared horseradish, peel and coarsely grate ¼ pound fresh horseradish root. Combine the grated horseradish, ½ tablespoon white wine vinegar, and ½ tablespoon water in a food processor. Season with kosher salt and pulse until smooth. Seal and store in the refrigerator for up to 2 months.

williams & graham bloody

SEAN KENYON, Williams & Graham, Denver, Colorado
GARNISH cornichon, pitted olive, and lime wheel

We Bloody enthusiasts owe massive praise to the pickle. I prefer a sweet and rich bite that unfolds into a tart and almost bitter finish— and a little dill never hurt my feelings. But can we take a moment and celebrate the Little Engine That Is Cornichon? I'd never had one until I was a grown adult, and I'm pretty sure if they were around when I was a kid I never would've left the kitchen table.

Colorado's Woody Creek Distillery makes an excellent single-distilled potato vodka, but try their gin, made with lemongrass, cranberries, grains of paradise, and the mad, beatific spirit of Hunter S. Thompson.

SERVES 1

2 OUNCES WOODY CREEK VODKA OR GIN

4 OUNCES WILLIAMS AND GRAHAM BLOODY MARY MIX (SEE RECIPE)

Combine the vodka and Bloody Mary mix in a highball glass filled with ice. Stir until chilled. Skewer a cornichon, olive, and lime wheel on a cocktail pick and garnish.

WILLIAMS AND GRAHAM BLOODY MARY MIX
MAKES 40 OUNCES, ENOUGH FOR 10 DRINKS

32 OUNCES TOMATO JUICE

4 OUNCES WORCESTERSHIRE SAUCE

2 OUNCES CORNICHON BRINE

2½ OUNCES FRESHLY SQUEEZED LEMON JUICE

1 TABLESPOON PREPARED HORSERADISH

1 TABLESPOON FRESHLY GROUND BLACK PEPPER

1 TABLESPOON SRIRACHA SAUCE

½ TABLESPOON GROUND CELERY SEED

½ TABLESPOON SALT

Combine all of the ingredients in a large pitcher. Store in a in a sealed container and refrigerate for up to 10 days.

the red wagon (virgin mary)

FARMER LEE JONES AND JAMIE SIMPSON, the Chef's Garden and Culinary Vegetable Institute, Milan, Ohio
GARNISH fresh chives and seasonal vegetables

Farmer Lee Jones, of the Chef's Garden and the Culinary Vegetable Institute, wears overalls and often has a hat on his head, but what makes him particularly distinguishable is his smile and warmth.

This Virgin Mary was created by chef Jamie Simpson. It's important to remember that every good host should have an option for nondrinkers.

One can't help but celebrate the frozen tomatoes that sub for everyday ice (see below). It evokes the garden theme of Farmer Lee's culinary foundations while paying homage to the wide spectrum of vegetable life found in and around Virgin Mary circles. Yes indeed, it's a fine teetotaler's delight.

SERVES 10

3½ POUNDS HEIRLOOM TOMATOES, DICED

1¼ CUPS DICED ONION

¾ CUP CHOPPED CELERY

5 OUNCES FRESHLY SQUEEZED LEMON JUICE

2½ OUNCES SHERRY VINEGAR

4½ TEASPOONS SALT

4½ TEASPOONS SWEET PAPRIKA

2½ TEASPOONS FRESHLY GROUND BLACK PEPPER

2½ TEASPOONS PREPARED HORSERADISH

1½ TEASPOONS CELERY SEEDS, TOASTED

8 TO 10 DASHES TABASCO SAUCE

TOMATO ICE CUBES (SEE NOTE)

Combine all of the ingredients except the Tomato Ice Cubes in a blender and blend until incredibly smooth. Pass through a fine-mesh strainer lined with cheesecloth or a coffee filter. Store in a sealed container and refrigerate for up to 1 week. To serve, pour 6 ounces over 3 or 4 Tomato Ice Cubes in a highball glass. Garnish with the chives so they stick out of the glass, and skewer the various vegetables to finish.

Note: To make Tomato Ice Cubes, in a food processor, blend 6 to 8 heirloom tomatoes until smooth, then pour into an ice cube tray, ideally with cubes no bigger than 1 inch. Freeze until frozen and store for up to 2 weeks.

red light

KEVIN DENTON, national mixologist, Pernod Ricard USA
GARNISH celery stalk

For as long as I have known him, Kevin Denton brings the thunder. When he's not performing music in one of three different bands, he's assembling thoughtful cocktails with Radiohead texture and Miles Davis creativity. Please enjoy drinking this version along with the Foo Fighters rocking classic "My Poor Brain," followed by the entire *Watch the Throne* album (refresh your beverage somewhere in the middle), and finishing with Adele's "Hello," coupled with a few sips of ice cold beer and peanut M&M's.

Kevin's spin on the classic incorporates nuanced Japanese ingredients, using rice vinegar and white miso, which elevates the umami wavelengths.

SERVES 1

2 OUNCES ABSOLUT VODKA

4 OUNCES RED LIGHT MIX (SEE RECIPE)

Combine the vodka and Red Light Mix in a cocktail shaker filled with ice. Roll the ingredients back and forth with another shaker 3 times and strain into a highball glass filled with ice. Garnish with a celery stalk.

RED LIGHT MIX
MAKES 40 OUNCES, ENOUGH FOR 10 DRINKS

36 OUNCES TOMATO JUICE	1 TABLESPOON WHITE MISO
½ CUP SLICED RED BELL PEPPER	1½ TEASPOONS FRESHLY GROUND BLACK PEPPER
1 OUNCE RICE VINEGAR	2 PINCHES CAYENNE PEPPER
1 OUNCE WORCESTERSHIRE SAUCE	

Combine all of the ingredients in a blender and blend until smooth. Store in a sealed container and refrigerate overnight to allow the flavors to integrate. The next day, pass through a fine-mesh strainer lined with cheesecloth or a coffee filter. Store in a sealed container and refrigerate for up to 2 weeks.

the cornballer

SEAN ROOT, Joseph Leonard, New York, New York
GARNISH baby heirloom yellow tomato (optional)

Every September, Joseph Leonard, our first restaurant, puts on Tomato Fest, a weeklong celebration of all things tomato. The food menu morphs into a tomato-licious extravaganza and people pile in from miles on end to experience the fruit-tastic magic.

The Cornballer comes back every year. It's not a difficult cocktail to build, but it definitely helps when using season-friendly sweet corn and tomatoes. Best to have a commercial juicer at your disposal if possible. And if you're using fresh lime and quality blanco tequila, cancel your dinner plans. You're with this drink for the long haul.

SERVES 1

MALDON SEA SALT, FOR THE RIM OF THE GLASS

1½ OUNCES CABEZA BLANCO TEQUILA

2 OUNCES SWEET CORN–YELLOW TOMATO JUICE (SEE RECIPE)

½ OUNCE AGAVE SYRUP

½ OUNCE FRESHLY SQUEEZED LIME JUICE

Coat the rim of a rocks glass with salt. Combine all of the remaining ingredients except the garnish in a cocktail shaker filled with ice. Shake until chilled and double-strain into the rimmed glass filled with ice. Garnish with a yellow baby heirloom tomato if you find them at your local grocer or farmers' market. Otherwise, any cherry tomato works well.

SWEET CORN–YELLOW TOMATO JUICE
MAKES 20 OUNCES, ENOUGH FOR 10 DRINKS

3 OR 4 EARS FRESH CORN   ABOUT 2 POUNDS YELLOW HEIRLOOM TOMATOES

Husk the corn and cut away the kernels with a long knife. Juice the tomatoes and corn separately, then combine them in a 3-to-1 tomato-to-corn ratio. (The amount of juice from tomatoes varies, so the yield is approximate.) Pass the tomato-corn mixture through a fine-mesh strainer lined with cheesecloth or a coffee filter. Store in a sealed container and refrigerate for up to 3 days.

danish mary

JOSEPH CONKLIN, Broder and Broder Nord, Portland, Oregon
GARNISH cherry tomato and assorted pickled vegetables
(optional)

Broder means "brother" in Swedish, and, brother, is this Bloody a keeper. (I would admittedly keep this around for any nonbrothers as well.)

As vodka's funky cousin, Aquavit has tremendous potential in cocktails, offering fennel and anise notes. A lot of the core ingredients (coriander, caraway, fennel, cumin, and citrus) used in making the spirit already have a place in culinary endeavors. Broder pickles everything from squash, blueberries, onions, cucumbers, peppers . . . the list goes on, depending on what's in season. It's Portland. Someone's always picklin' something!

Joe was a little worried about sharing this recipe with the world, but the world needs it, Joe! We already have enough superhero movies. Let's make this Mary the new superhero.

SERVES 1

CELERY SEEDS, FOR THE RIM OF THE GLASS (OPTIONAL)

CELERY SALT, FOR THE RIM OF THE GLASS (OPTIONAL)

COARSE SEA SALT, FOR THE RIM OF THE GLASS (OPTIONAL)

2 OUNCES KROGSTAD AQUAVIT, LINIE AQUAVIT, OR SVEDKA VODKA

8 OUNCES DANISH MARY MIX (PAGE 112)

Mix the celery seeds, celery salt, and salt together on a small plate. Coat the rim of a pint glass with the salt mixture. Combine the aquavit and Danish Mary Mix in a cocktail shaker filled with ice. Roll the ingredients back and forth with another shaker 3 times. Fill the glass with ice and strain the cocktail into it. Garnish with a cherry tomato and pickled vegetables.

DANISH MARY MIX

MAKES 2 QUARTS, ENOUGH FOR 8 DRINKS

1½ TEASPOONS CELERY SEEDS

1½ TEASPOONS FENNEL SEEDS

1½ TEASPOONS DILL SEEDS

1½ TEASPOONS CUMIN SEEDS

1½ TEASPOONS RED PEPPER FLAKES

½ BUNCH DILL, CHOPPED

3 OUNCES PORTER OR GUINNESS STOUT

3 OUNCES TOMATO PASTE

¼ CUP PREPARED HORSERADISH

2 OUNCES FRESHLY SQUEEZED LEMON JUICE

1 OUNCE WORCESTERSHIRE SAUCE

1½ TEASPOONS GARLIC POWDER

1½ TEASPOONS CELERY SALT

1½ TEASPOONS FRESHLY GROUND BLACK PEPPER

¾ TEASPOON GROUND CUMIN

¾ TEASPOON MILD CURRY POWDER

½ TEASPOON CAYENNE PEPPER

50 OUNCES TOMATO JUICE (PREFERABLY ORGANIC)

In a nonstick sauté pan over medium heat, toast the celery seeds, fennel seeds, dill seeds, and cumin seeds just until fragrant, about 3 minutes. Let cool. Combine the toasted seeds, red pepper flakes, and dill in a cheesecloth sachet and set aside.

In a 2-quart sealable container, combine all of the remaining ingredients except the tomato juice. Add the sachet of spices and herbs, mix well, and pour in the tomato juice. Stir to blend. Seal the container and refrigerate for at least 1 day, to allow the flavors to integrate, and up to 1 week. Remove the sachet after 1 day. Mix well before using.

wake and bacon bloody mary

CRAIG CHRISTOPHER, Beer Kitchen, Kansas City, Missouri
GARNISH cooked strip of thick-cut bacon, celery stalk, pitted olive, and lemon wedge

As my friend Chef Bill would say, "If I could wrap the world in bacon, I would do it."

Barbecue-soaked Kansas City's Beer Kitchen is known for some unbelievable Bloody Marys: the Cajun Mary, the Beefeater Mary (featuring a smoked beef stick), and the Wake and Bacon Bloody Mary recipe here. If you've been waiting for a bacon vodka recipe, this is it. And you only need the fat to make the vodka. Keep the bacon for yourself and any well-behaved loved ones.

SERVES 1

2 OUNCES BACON-INFUSED VODKA (PAGE 155)

5 OUNCES WAKE AND BACON BLOODY MARY MIX (SEE RECIPE)

Combine the vodka and Bloody mix in a cocktail shaker filled with ice. Roll the ingredients back and forth with another shaker 3 times and strain into a pint glass filled with ice. Garnish with bacon, a celery stalk, an olive, and a lemon wedge.

WAKE AND BACON BLOODY MARY MIX
MAKES 2 QUARTS, ENOUGH FOR 12 DRINKS

56 OUNCES SACRAMENTO TOMATO JUICE

2½ OUNCES WORCESTERSHIRE SAUCE

2 OUNCES CHOLULA HOT SAUCE

1½ OUNCES FRESHLY SQUEEZED LEMON JUICE

1½ OUNCES FRESHLY SQUEEZED LIME JUICE

1½ TEASPOONS CELERY SALT

1½ TEASPOONS STEAK SEASONING

¾ TEASPOON FRESHLY GROUND BLACK PEPPER

¾ TEASPOON PREPARED HORSERADISH

¾ TEASPOON TOMATO PASTE

Combine all of the ingredients in a large pitcher. Store in a in a sealed container and refrigerate for up to 10 days.

denman street mary

LAUREN MOTE, bar consultant, Vancouver, Canada
GARNISH 2 tablespoons Pickled Thread-Slaw, drained (page 117)

Lauren Mote doesn't mess around. Girl. Crushes. It. Not only is she a partner in Bittered Sling Bitters, a terrific bitters company based out of Vancouver, but she was also *Vancouver Magazine*'s 2015 Bartender of the Year and Diageo's Bartender of the Year World Class Canada 2015. Lauren uses the one-two knockout punch of Don Julio tequila and Vida mezcal here. The tequila serenades you with its notes of white pepper, citrus, and honeyed spice, while the mezcal pulls you toward the dance floor with smoke and cinnamon.

There's a healthy (pun intended) amount of fresh juices in this recipe. I highly recommend a Vitamix or commercial juicer.

If you can source the Moondog Bitters, great, or try Hella Chili Bitters, Bitterman's Hellfire Habanero Bitters, or another spicy, earthy, aromatic bitters option.

SERVES 1

CHIVE AND TARRAGON SALT, FOR THE RIM OF THE GLASS (PAGE 154)

1 OUNCE DON JULIO REPOSADO TEQUILA

1 OUNCE DEL MAGUEY VIDA MEZCAL

4 OUNCES RED MIX (PAGE 117)

2 DASHES BITTERED SLING MOONDOG BITTERS

Coat the rim of a collins glass with chive and tarragon salt. Combine all of the remaining ingredients except the garnish in a cocktail shaker filled with ice. Roll back and forth with another shaker 3 times. Fill the rimmed glass with ice and strain the cocktail into it, leaving 1 inch of room at the top. Float the Pickled Thread-Slaw on top and serve with a straw.

RED MIX

MAKES 40 OUNCES, ENOUGH FOR 10 DRINKS

28 OUNCES WHOLE PEELED SAN MARZANO TOMATOES	½ TEASPOON BLACK MUSTARD POWDER
3 OUNCES CARROT JUICE	¼ TEASPOON GROUND FENUGREEK POWDER
3 OUNCES CUCUMBER JUICE	
3 OUNCES CELERY JUICE	¼ TEASPOON SWEET SMOKED PAPRIKA
2 OUNCES FRESHLY SQUEEZED LEMON JUICE	¼ TEASPOON SALT
1½ OUNCES SIMPLE SYRUP	¼ TEASPOON FRESHLY GROUND BLACK PEPPER
1 SMALL DRIED ANCHO CHILE PEPPER	

Combine all of the ingredients in a blender and blend until smooth. Pass through a fine-mesh strainer. Store in a sealed container and refrigerate for up to 7 days.

PICKLED THREAD-SLAW

MAKES 2 CUPS

½ ENGLISH CUCUMBER, UNPEELED	½ CUP SUGAR
1 CELERY STALK	½ CUP SALT
1 LIME, SCRUBBED	¼ CUP SHERRY VINEGAR

Cut the cucumber and celery into thin matchsticks. Using the edge of a channel knife, cut the lime peel into matchstick-size threads. Combine the cucumber, celery, and lime peel in a jar.

Combine the sugar, salt, and vinegar in a small saucepan and warm over medium heat until the sugar and salt dissolve. Pour the pickling liquid over the threads. Seal the jar and refrigerate for up to 1 month.

the gilda'd mary

KEVIN PATRICIO, La Madame, San Sebastián, Spain
GARNISH anchovy-stuffed olive, pickled Basque
guindilla peppers (optional), and lime twist

Kevin's recipe pays homage to the Gilda, the original Basque pintxo (the Basque version of tapas), which is an olive, a guindilla pepper, and a salted anchovy on a toothpick, served over the top as this Bloody's garnish. Gildas were named after *Gilda*, the 1946 movie starring screen icon Rita Hayworth.

Pintxo comes from *pinchar*—"to pierce"—which we know is a movement commonly associated with Bloody Mary garnishes. So it would seem pintxos and Bloody Marys both followed Rita Hayworth's dance moves in knocking people off their feet.

SERVES 1

2 OUNCES TITO'S VODKA

4 OUNCES GILDA'D MARIE MIX (SEE RECIPE)

1 OUNCE FRESHLY SQUEEZED LIME JUICE

EXTRA-VIRGIN OLIVE OIL

FRESHLY GROUND BLACK PEPPER

Combine the vodka, mix, and lime juice in a cocktail shaker filled with ice. Roll the ingredients back and forth with another shaker 3 times and strain into a Basque cider or highball glass filled with ice. Garnish with a skewered anchovy-stuffed olive, a guindilla pepper, and a lime twist. Drizzle olive oil over the garnishes and top with the black pepper.

GILDA'D MARIE MIX

MAKES 40 OUNCES, ENOUGH FOR 10 DRINKS

30 OUNCES SACRAMENTO TOMATO JUICE

3½ OUNCES FRANK'S REDHOT SAUCE

3½ OUNCES WORCESTERSHIRE SAUCE

2 OUNCES FRESHLY GRATED HORSERADISH

1 OUNCE BALSAMIC VINEGAR

¾ TEASPOON COARSELY GROUND BLACK PEPPER

¾ TEASPOON FINE SEA SALT

¾ TEASPOON CELERY SALT

Combine all of the ingredients in a large pitcher. Store in a sealed container and refrigerate for up to 2 weeks.

mary go round

BRIAN BARTELS, New York, New York

GARNISH cucumber wheel or watermelon radish with
a dab of Sriracha sauce, chile oil, or Tabasco sauce;
fresh sprig of dill

The biggest star in this Bloody Mary is the garnish. A fresh, fragrant
dill sprig, aromatic cucumber, or aesthetically pleasing watermelon
radish floating in the cocktail and sprinkled with seasoning will look
great. The classic Bloody Mary wasn't too fussy, and neither is this
version. If you don't have St. George Green Chile vodka, go for regular
vodka, gin, sake, rum, spicy red wine, grappa, aquavit, tequila, or
sherry. Go for what makes you feel good!

SERVES 1

1½ OUNCES VODKA,
PREFERABLY ST. GEORGE
GREEN CHILE VODKA

1½ OUNCES
TOMATO JUICE

¼ OUNCE FRESHLY
SQUEEZED LEMON JUICE

SPICES AND SEASONINGS
TO YOUR LIKING

Combine the vodka, tomato juice, and lemon juice in
a cocktail shaker filled with ice. Roll the ingredients
back and forth with another shaker 3 times and
strain into a chilled coupe or martini glass. Slice a
cucumber ⅛ inch thick or thinly slice watermelon
radish in the shape of a wheel, add the spices and
seasonings of your choice, and float in the glass.

kimchee and nori bloody mary

MARISA AND KEN HO, Lucky Luna, Brooklyn, New York
GARNISH 1 large piece kimchee and 2 or 3 nori strips

Husband and wife super-duo Marisa and Ken have won Bloody Mary contests for their delectable Bloodys. They have a tasty little corner restaurant in Greenpoint, Brooklyn, called Lucky Luna, that serves a cross between Mexican and Taiwanese cuisine. You couldn't ask for two nicer people to make you feel at home. Thanks to kimchee, this Bloody's got an extra kick of spicy heat to keep you warm—not to mention healthy vitamins. Kimchee's got As, Bs, and Cs. Drink this cocktail, get good grades, and stay healthy!

SERVES 1

SALT, FOR THE RIM OF THE GLASS

1½ OUNCES VODKA

5 OUNCES LUCKY LUNA BLOODY MARY MIX (PAGE 121)

¾ OUNCE FRESHLY SQUEEZED LEMON JUICE

½ OUNCE KIMCHEE PUREE (SEE NOTE)

Coat the rim of a pint glass with salt. Combine all of the ingredients except the garnish in a cocktail shaker filled with ice. Roll the ingredients back and forth with another shaker 3 times. Fill the rimmed glass with ice and strain the cocktail into it. Garnish with the kimchee and nori.

Note: To make kimchee puree, place any store-bought kimchee and a small amount of canola oil in a blender and pulse until a paste forms. If it's still thick, add a touch more canola oil. The goal is to find a consistency between ketchup and salsa.

LUCKY LUNA BLOODY MARY MIX

MAKES 50 OUNCES, ENOUGH FOR 10 DRINKS

38 OUNCES TOMATO JUICE

5 OUNCES VALENTINA OR OTHER HOT SAUCE

3 OUNCES SRIRACHA SAUCE

3 OUNCES WORCESTERSHIRE SAUCE

1 OUNCE MAGGI SEASONING SAUCE

3 TABLESPOONS PREPARED HORSERADISH

2½ TEASPOONS SALT

2½ TEASPOONS FRESHLY GROUND BLACK PEPPER

Combine all of the ingredients in a large pitcher. Store in a sealed container and refrigerate for up to 1 week.

beet and sherry bloody mary

LEO ROBITSCHEK, the NoMad and Eleven Madison Park,
New York, New York
GARNISH lemon wedge and celery stalk

Leo Robitschek makes me drink. Anyone who can do that is either a true friend or a family member. To know Leo is to know he fits into both categories. He also consistently creates some of the most well-balanced, well-executed, unpretentious yet praiseworthy cocktails around. Though he may not carry a scholastic degree in medicine, Dr. Leo's menus surgically engage the history and influence of craft cocktail appreciation, oft followed by an impromptu dance party.

Amontillado sherry and beet juice play very well together here. It's a welcome curveball, followed by a tasty home run.

SERVES 1

2 OUNCES
AMONTILLADO SHERRY

6 OUNCES BEET MARY
MIX (SEE RECIPE)

Combine the sherry and Beet Mary Mix in a cocktail shaker filled with ice. Roll the ingredients back and forth with another shaker 3 times and strain into a highball glass filled with ice. Garnish with a lemon wedge and celery stalk.

BEET MARY MIX
MAKES 60 OUNCES, ENOUGH FOR 10 DRINKS

44 OUNCES TOMATO JUICE

8 OUNCES BEET JUICE

4 OUNCES WORCESTERSHIRE
SAUCE

2 OUNCES TABASCO SAUCE

1 OUNCE MAGGI
SEASONING SAUCE

2 TEASPOONS SALT

2 TEASPOONS FRESHLY
GROUND BLACK PEPPER

Combine all of the ingredients in a large pitcher. Store in a sealed container and refrigerate for up to 1 week.

michael and vito

JACK HARRIS, Perla Cafe, New York, New York
GARNISH cherry tomato and fresh basil leaf

This recipe reminds me of the importance of experimentation. Chef Jack Harris happened upon a container full of fresh tomato water and used his creativity and extensive training in Italian cooking to make this beauty. Tomato water is the translucent water within each tomato fruit, with fresh, light, and vibrant tomato flavor. It was invented by people who have all the time in the world. Tomato water takes time and patience to extract. The pureed ingredients within a tomato need to drip-drain through a cheesecloth, so for Chef Jack to see some fresh tomato water taking up space on a shelf is like Indiana Jones tripping over the Lost Ark on his way to the fedora store.

Serve one up for a friend. As Marlon Brando says in *The Godfather,* "I'm gonna make him a Bloody he can't refuse."

SERVES 1

1 OUNCE FORDS GIN

1 OUNCE BIANCO VERMOUTH, PREFERABLY CARPANO BIANCO

½ OUNCE CHEF JACK'S TOMATO WATER (SEE RECIPE)

Combine all of the ingredients except the garnish in a mixing glass filled with ice. Stir until chilled and strain into a Nick and Nora glass. Skewer the cherry tomato and basil leaf on a cocktail pick and garnish.

CHEF JACK'S TOMATO WATER
MAKES 6 OUNCES, ENOUGH FOR 10 DRINKS

3 ROMA TOMATOES	3 OR 4 FRESH BASIL LEAVES
½ SHALLOT	1 TABLESPOON SALT
1 CLOVE GARLIC	¼ CUP CHAMPAGNE VINEGAR

Quarter the Roma tomatoes and place in a food processor. Add all of the remaining ingredients to the food processor and pulse until coarsely chopped. Pass through a fine-mesh strainer lined with cheesecloth or a coffee filter. Taste and adjust the seasoning. Store in a sealed container and refrigerate for up to 1 week.

normandie bloody mary

DEVON TARBY, the Normandie Club, Los Angeles, California
GARNISH 2 cherry tomatoes and a lemon wedge

While scouring the Internet for some inspiration for our restaurants' bars, one image stuck with me: that of Devon Tarby's Normandie Club Bloody Mary. A tall, narrow highball glass with an almost frosted exterior, with two luscious cherry tomatoes and a lemon wedge on top—simple, elegant, regal. Drop the mic. Boom goes the dynamite.

SERVES 1

SALT, FOR THE RIM OF THE GLASS (OPTIONAL)

FRESHLY GROUND BLACK PEPPER, FOR THE RIM OF THE GLASS (OPTIONAL)

1½ OUNCES KROGSTAD AQUAVIT

4 OUNCES NORMANDIE BLOODY MARY MIX (SEE RECIPE)

¼ OUNCE FRESHLY SQUEEZED LEMON JUICE

¼ OUNCE FRESHLY SQUEEZED LIME JUICE

Mix the salt and pepper together on a small plate. Coat half of the rim of a highball glass with the mixture. Combine all of the remaining ingredients except the garnish in a mixing glass filled with ice. Stir until chilled and strain into the rimmed glass. Skewer the cherry tomatoes on a cocktail pick. Garnish with the tomatoes and a lemon wedge.

NORMANDIE BLOODY MARY MIX

MAKES ABOUT 40 OUNCES, ENOUGH FOR 10 DRINKS

20 OUNCES FRESH TOMATO JUICE

5 OUNCES FRESH CELERY JUICE

4 OUNCES FRESH RED BELL PEPPER JUICE

2½ OUNCES TOMATO BOUILLON CONCENTRATE

1¼ OUNCES FRESHLY SQUEEZED LEMON JUICE

1¼ OUNCES FRESHLY SQUEEZED LIME JUICE

1¼ OUNCES BUBBIES PICKLE BRINE

3 TABLESPOONS WORCESTERSHIRE SAUCE

1½ TABLESPOONS BRAGG LIQUID AMINOS

1½ TABLESPOONS SRIRACHA SAUCE

1½ TABLESPOONS BUBBIES PREPARED HORSERADISH

Combine all of the ingredients in a large pitcher. Refrigerate in a sealed container for up to 1 week.

east indies bloody mary

JACOB GRIER, cocktail consultant, Portland, Oregon
GARNISH grilled prawn (see note); various pickled vegetables
such as green beans, cucumber, or cauliflower (see page 151)

Jacob Grier writes a damn fine blog (jacobgrier.com/blog) on the expansive world of cocktails and how we interact with them. You can count on his posts being well researched and full of information on new spirits, concoctions, coffee, economics, magic, useful Internet tools, and weird sea creatures. Pretty much all of the same conversations you have at brunch while drinking Bloody Marys.

Batavia arrack is an Indonesian spirit from the island of Java, distilled from sugarcane and red rice, that has flavors of citrus and chocolate. It's no surprise that the spirit was used in early punch recipes. Punches and Bloody Marys have always been buddies on the cocktail playground.

SERVES 1

1 PINCH SALT

1 PINCH GROUND CUMIN

1½ OUNCES BATAVIA ARRACK

4 OUNCES EAST INDIES BLOODY MARY MIX (PAGE 129)

2 TEASPOONS INDONESIAN SPICE PASTE (PAGE 129)

Mix the salt and cumin together on a small plate. Coat the rim of a pint glass with the salt mixture. Combine the Batavia arrack, Bloody Mary mix, and spice paste in a cocktail shaker filled with ice. Roll the ingredients back and forth with another shaker 3 times. Fill the rimmed glass with ice and strain the cocktail into it. Go crazy with the garnishes.

Note: To grill the prawn, lightly toss 1 shell-on shrimp in extra-virgin olive oil and season with kosher salt and freshly ground black pepper. Place on a grill pan or griddle over high heat and grill for 2 minutes on each side or until pink and opaque.

EAST INDIES BLOODY MARY MIX

MAKES 40 OUNCES, ENOUGH FOR 10 DRINKS

35 OUNCES TOMATO JUICE	4 TEASPOONS TABASCO SAUCE, OR TO TASTE
3 OUNCES FRESHLY SQUEEZED LEMON JUICE	2 TEASPOONS SALT
2 TABLESPOONS PREPARED HORSERADISH	1 TEASPOON GROUND CELERY SEED
4 TEASPOONS WORCESTERSHIRE SAUCE	½ TEASPOON FRESHLY GROUND BLACK PEPPER

Combine all of the ingredients, in a large pitcher. Store in a sealed container and refrigerate for up to 1 week.

INDONESIAN SPICE PASTE

MAKES ½ CUP, ENOUGH FOR 10 DRINKS

¼ CUP SAMBAL OELEK	½ TEASPOON GROUND TURMERIC
2 TABLESPOONS FISH SAUCE	½ TEASPOON GROUND CUMIN
½ TEASPOON GROUND NUTMEG	

Combine all of the ingredients in a small bowl. Store in a sealed container in a cool, dark place for up to 1 week.

underground food collective maria

MARK BYSTROM AND JONNY HUNTER, Underground Food Collective, Madison, Wisconsin
GARNISH sliced pepperoni, culatello, or other cured meats

Jonny Hunter and the merry gang of the Underground Food Collective have been changing the culinary landscape of Wisconsin one landjäger encasing at a time (sorry for my sausage puns).

White soy sauce, Dijon, and the delectable Chicago-based Co-op Batsauce (a hot sauce) are some ingredients one rarely associates with Bloodys. If you can't get your hands on their Batsauce, substitute Sriracha or Tabasco sauce.

SERVES 1

1½ OUNCES BLANCO TEQUILA

5 OUNCES UNDERGROUND BLOODY MARIA MIX (SEE RECIPE)

Combine the tequila and Bloody mix in a cocktail shaker filled with ice. Roll the ingredients back and forth with another shaker 3 times and strain into an old-fashioned glass filled with ice. Garnish with a pepperoni ribbon and a culatello flower.

UNDERGROUND BLOODY MARIA MIX
MAKES 50 OUNCES, ENOUGH FOR 10 DRINKS

36 OUNCES TOMATO WATER (PAGE 75)

4½ OUNCES WHITE SHOYU SOY SAUCE

4½ OUNCES CORNICHON BRINE

3½ OUNCES FRESHLY SQUEEZED LEMON JUICE

¼ CUP DIJON MUSTARD

3 TABLESPOONS CO-OP BATSAUCE

2 TABLESPOONS PREPARED HORSERADISH

2 TEASPOONS SALT

2 TEASPOON FRESHLY GROUND BLACK PEPPER

Combine all of the ingredients in a large pitcher and refrigerate overnight to allow the flavors to integrate. Store in a sealed container and refrigerate for up to 3 days.

the shanty's red snapper

NATE DUMAS, The Shanty at New York Distilling,
Brooklyn, New York
GARNISH Castelvetrano olive and lemon wedge

This recipe invokes Fernand "Pete" Petiot's classic Red Snapper (page 53), with some added boost from amontillado sherry, a nutty, approachable, and delicious sherry made only in Spain that's fortunately available in many U.S. stores. Chief Gowanus gin (which starts as a rye, incorporating spice, vanilla, and citrus, then returns to a copper pot still for the juniper effect) applies a richness and texture as a terrific spirit choice. The coup de grace is the best olive in the world, the Kermit-green Castelvetrano, as a garnish. The recipe calls for one, but keep many nearby, as they're worth the company. Just don't make Miss Piggy mad!

SERVES 1

1½ OUNCES CHIEF
GOWANUS GIN

4 OUNCES RED SNAPPER
MIX (SEE RECIPE)

Combine the gin and Red Snapper Mix in a cocktail shaker filled with ice. Roll the ingredients back and forth with another shaker 3 times and strain into a highball glass filled with ice. Skewer the olive and lemon wedge on a cocktail pick and garnish.

RED SNAPPER MIX

MAKES 1⅓ QUARTS, ENOUGH FOR 10 DRINKS

36 OUNCES TOMATO JUICE

4 OUNCES
AMONTILLADO SHERRY

1½ OUNCES
WORCESTERSHIRE SAUCE

¾ OUNCE TABASCO SAUCE

¾ TEASPOON CELERY SALT

½ TEASPOON FRESHLY
GROUND BLACK PEPPER

Combine all of the ingredients in a large pitcher. Store in a sealed container and refrigerate for up to 10 days.

barbecue bloody mary

CHRIS LILLY, Big Bob Gibson's Bar-B-Q, Decatur, Alabama
GARNISH Grilled Lemons, Jalapeño Skewers, and/or
Pickle Spears (page 137)

Chris Lilly has been at the helm of Big Bob Gibson's Bar-B-Q in Decatur, Alabama, for some time now, constantly perfecting and producing quintessential barbecue goodness. I had the chance to try Chris's barbecue at the Big Apple Barbecue Block Party in 2011, and I can honestly say it has forever changed me. I compare all barbecue I have eaten since against his majestic mountaintop of flavor. Hope you feel the same about his Bloody, featuring beef jus (save the drippings from your next barbecue, or use unsalted beef broth), smoked celery salt, and lotsa smiles and high fives.

SERVES 10

64 OUNCES TOMATO JUICE

20 OUNCES VODKA

1½ CUPS BEEF DRIPPINGS (OR BEEF BROTH)

5 TABLESPOONS WORCESTERSHIRE SAUCE

2 TEASPOONS PREPARED HORSERADISH

2 TEASPOONS SRIRACHA SAUCE

1½ TEASPOONS CELERY SALT

1½ TEASPOONS FRESHLY GROUND BLACK PEPPER

2½ TEASPOONS SALT

JUICE OF ½ HALF LEMON

In a large pitcher, combine the tomato juice, vodka, beef drippings, Worcestershire, horseradish, Sriracha, ½ teaspoon of the celery salt, and the pepper. Squeeze the juice from 1 lemon half into the pitcher, stir well, and refrigerate until chilled.

Run the remaining lemon halves around the rim of 10 highball glasses. Combine the remaining 1 teaspoon celery salt and kosher salt on a small plate. Coat the rims of the glasses with the salt mixture. Fill the rimmed glasses with the chilled Bloody Mary and ice, garnish as desired, and serve.

GRILLED LEMONS, JALAPEÑO SKEWERS, AND PICKLE SPEARS

MAKES ENOUGH FOR 10 DRINKS

1½ TABLESPOONS SUGAR	5 JALAPEÑO CHILES
5 LEMONS, HALVED	10 DILL PICKLE SPEARS

Prepare a charcoal fire to medium-high heat or preheat a gas grill to 450°F. While the grill is heating, put the sugar on a plate and twist the face of each lemon half into the sugar. Place the lemon halves facedown on the grill and grill until the sugar caramelizes, about 2 minutes. Remove from the grill and set aside. Wear disposable gloves when handling the jalapeños and avoid touching your face. Cut off the tops, cut in half and remove the seeds and veins with a tiny spoon. Grill the jalapeños until they're charred, approximately 4 minutes on each side. Pickles are far easier. If grilling, lay them down flat across the ribs of the grill over medium heat for 30 to 60 seconds, flipping when they slightly char.

pirate mary

BRIAN BARTELS, New York, New York
GARNISH slice of pineapple, lime wheel,
and pineapple leaf or celery stalk, plus
2 turns of freshly ground black pepper

I have always proclaimed that my favorite parts about the *Pirates of the Caribbean* films have been Keira Knightley, and apart from the obvious reasons, her character is interesting because we know right off the bat how badly she wants to be a pirate.

This spin-off has got my sweet tooth in mind. I love coconut water, fresh pineapple juice, yellow tomatoes, and, you guessed it, great rum! Please note that you will have to break out a nice juicer to acquire these fresh ingredients. The pineapple steps out upon first sipping, while the pepper does a fine job of balancing the back end by drying out the cloying sweetness.

Swashbuckle this already. It's a Bloody good mutiny!

SERVES 1

1½ OUNCES BANKS
5 ISLAND RUM

2½ OUNCES PIRATE
MARY MIX (SEE RECIPE)

4 TURNS OF FRESHLY
GROUND BLACK PEPPER

3 DASHES BITTER TRUTH
CELERY BITTERS

Combine all of the ingredients except the garnishes in a cocktail shaker filled with ice. Roll the ingredients back and forth with another shaker 3 times and strain into a rocks glass filled with ice. Garnish with a pineapple slice, lime wheel, pineapple leaf, and pepper.

PIRATE MARY MIX
MAKES 3 CUPS, ENOUGH TO SERVE 10 SCALAWAGS

10 OUNCES COCONUT WATER

10 OUNCES YELLOW
TOMATO JUICE

4½ OUNCES FRESH
PINEAPPLE JUICE

Combine the coconut water, tomato juice, and pineapple juice in a large pitcher. Store in a sealed container and refrigerate for up to 2 days.

all-day bloody mary

NAREN YOUNG, Dante, New York, New York
GARNISH skewer of peperoncini, cherry tomato, and
cornichon; cucumber wheel (optional); grated horseradish
PICTURED opposite title page (page ii)

Located on historic MacDougal Street in Manhattan, Dante has been a New York institution for many years; it originally opened as Caffé Dante circa 1915, and in 2015, the current owners abbreviated the longer title to Dante. It once kept Bob Dylan warm, introduced countless poems and literature from the Beat Generation, and fed many other artists and Greenwich Villagers seeking solace from the everyday breakneck pace of New York. It's refreshing to know the history of spaces in New York continues to this day, and Naren has celebrated that tradition with his new version of Caffé Dante, which is one of my favorite places to drink in New York.

Be ready to juice a lot for this recipe—but rest assured, it's worth it. Naren's vitamin-packed Bloody Mary is always fresh and available all day, every day, anytime you stop by Dante on MacDougal Street, for a drink or a bite or a memory, whether it be new or old. Pastis is a welcome ingredient in Bloody Mary circles and has been appearing in new recipes in recent years.

SERVES 1

FENNEL SALT, FOR THE
RIM OF THE GLASS
(PAGE 154)

1½ OUNCES AYLESBURY
DUCK VODKA

¼ OUNCE PERNOD
PASTIS

5 OUNCES DANTE MARY
MIX (PAGE 141)

2 DASHES RED
TABASCO SAUCE

2 DASHES GREEN
TABASCO SAUCE

Coat the rim of a highball glass with the fennel salt. Fill the rimmed glass with ice and add all of the remaining ingredients except the garnish. Stir until chilled. Skewer the pepperoncini, cherry tomato, and cornichon on a cocktail pick and garnish, along with the cucumber wheel. Sprinkle a pinch of horseradish over the top.

DANTE MARY MIX

MAKES 60 OUNCES, ENOUGH FOR 10 DRINKS

¼ CUP FRESHLY SQUEEZED LEMON JUICE

2 TEASPOONS TOMATO PASTE

32 OUNCES FRESH TOMATO JUICE

½ CUP FRESH CARROT JUICE

½ CUP FRESH CELERY JUICE

½ CUP FRESH FENNEL JUICE

½ CUP FRESH CUCUMBER JUICE

½ CUP FRESH RED BELL PEPPER JUICE

1 TABLESPOON MALDON SEA SALT

1 TABLESPOON CELERY SALT

1 TABLESPOON FRESHLY GROUND BLACK PEPPER

1¼ OUNCES WORCESTERSHIRE SAUCE

In a small bowl, stir together the lemon juice and tomato paste until the tomato paste dissolves. Combine the lemon juice mixture with all of the remaining ingredients in a large pitcher. Store in a sealed container and refrigerate for up to 3 days.

state street bloody mary

BRIAN BARTELS, New York, New York
GARNISH slice of summer sausage, Benny's Bloody Mary
Beef Straw, or any seasoned, cured meats

Before I started working there with Jim Meehan and serving Guinness to Gabriel Stulman, Paul's Club was the bar I drank in all the time. Imagine getting a job at your dream bar, where you can then drink for free! Paul's is located on State Street in Madison, Wisconsin, a street far too inspiring to ignore. This recipe is my homage.

SERVES 1

SALT, FOR THE RIM OF THE GLASS

FRESHLY GROUND BLACK PEPPER, FOR THE RIM OF THE GLASS

1½ OUNCES DEATH'S DOOR VODKA, MEZCAL, TEQUILA, GIN, OR WHITE WHISKEY

5 OUNCES STATE STREET BLOODY MARY MIX (SEE RECIPE)

SNIT OF BEER, PREFERABLY NEW GLARUS SPOTTED COW (SEE NOTE, PAGE 90)

Mix the salt and pepper together on a small plate, and coat half of the rim of a highball glass with the mixture. Combine the vodka and Bloody mix in a cocktail shaker filled with ice. Roll the ingredients back and forth with another shaker 3 times. Fill the rimmed glass with ice and strain the cocktail into it. Garnish with the summer sausage or an alternate beefalicious option. If you're lucky enough to be in Wisconsin, serve a New Glarus Spotted Cow for your snit.

STATE STREET BLOODY MARY MIX

MAKES 50 OUNCES, ENOUGH FOR 10 COCKTAILS

44 OUNCES TOMATO JUICE

2 OUNCES DEL MAGUEY VIDA MEZCAL OR OTHER INEXPENSIVE MEZCAL

2 OUNCES WORCESTERSHIRE SAUCE

1 OUNCE TABASCO CHIPOTLE SAUCE

½ OUNCE SOY SAUCE

½ OUNCE SRIRACHA SAUCE

1 TABLESPOON MOLASSES

1 TABLESPOON OLD BAY SEASONING

1¼ TEASPOONS CELERY SEEDS

1 TEASPOON CRACKED BLACK PEPPER

¾ TEASPOON GROUND WHITE PEPPER

Combine the ingredients in a large pitcher. Store in a sealed container and refrigerate for up to 2 weeks.

morgenthaler mary

JEFFREY MORGENTHALER, Clyde Common,
· Portland, Oregon
GARNISH whatever your heart desires (see note)

Young (and old!) bartenders of the world, if you ever want to truly embrace what makes a bartender unforgettable, treat your strangers as old friends, always hold open doors for others, and be unendingly fair. Watching Jeff Morgenthaler inhabit these traits is to watch an artist with a paintbrush as they Bob Ross a canvas. Yes, Bob Ross is a verb. Just like Morgenthaler should be a verb. Try it: "How can I Morgenthaler this?" Jeff has found this recipe works best when it's allowed to sit overnight so the flavors coalesce. Best to try and make the night before.

SERVES 1

⅛ TEASPOON SALT, FOR THE RIM OF THE GLASS (OPTIONAL)

2 OUNCES VODKA

6 OUNCES MORGENTHALER MIX (PAGE 145)

Coat the rim of a pint glass with salt and fill with ice. Add the vodka and top off with the mix. Stir until chilled. Garnish as you like.

Note: Jeffrey encourages you to mix and match from any of the following: a celery stalk, stuffed olives, cornichons, pickled white asparagus, a lemon wedge, a lime wedge, pearl onions, pickled green beans, cherry tomatoes, pickled garlic cloves, and peperoncini.

MORGENTHALER MIX

MAKES 60 OUNCES, ENOUGH FOR 10 DRINKS

55 OUNCES TOMATO JUICE

¾ SMALL AVOCADO

1 CLOVE GARLIC, MINCED

2½ OUNCES
WORCESTERSHIRE SAUCE

1¾ OUNCES FRESHLY
SQUEEZED LEMON JUICE

1¾ TABLESPOONS
STEAK SAUCE

1 TABLESPOON FRESHLY
GROUND BLACK PEPPER

1¾ TEASPOONS CELERY SALT

1¾ TEASPOONS HOT SAUCE

1½ TEASPOONS PREPARED
HORSERADISH

Combine 8 ounces of the tomato juice, the avocado, and the garlic in a food processor or blender and process until smooth. Combine with all of the remaining ingredients in a large pitcher. Store in a sealed container and refrigerate for at least 1 day, to allow the flavors to integrate. Store for up to 1 week.

bloody mary no. 20

DANIEL TRUJILLO AND GABRIEL STULMAN, Joseph Leonard
and Jeffrey's Grocery, New York, New York
GARNISH lemon wedge, cornichon, and olive

We treat brunch with great respect, privilege, and enthusiasm at each of our Happy Cooking Hospitality restaurants. Bloody Mary No. 20 has been steadily holding the brunch fort at Joseph Leonard and Jeffrey's Grocery since we opened their doors, and keeps on scoring big points with the masses. Daniel Trujillo is a terrific example of how those restaurants have flourished. Daniel has worked with us for nearly ten years now, and his capacity to learn and grow in our work environment knows no equal.

The No. 20 was not our twentieth version of the recipe, but Gabriel wanted to name this one after legendary Detroit Lion football player Barry Sanders. As Gabriel is apt to happily proclaim, "He never falls down!" We only hope the same for you.

SERVES 1

2 OUNCES PLAIN VODKA, CILANTRO-INFUSED VODKA (PAGE 156), OR DILL-INFUSED VODKA (PAGE 156)

3 OUNCES BLOODY MARY NO. 20 MIX (SEE RECIPE)

6 OUNCES PILSNER BEER

Combine the vodka and Bloody mix in a cocktail shaker filled with ice. Roll the ingredients back and forth with another shaker 3 times and strain into a rocks glass filled with ice. Garnish with an olive, cornichon, and lemon wedge. Serve with a beer shorty.

BLOODY MARY NO. 20 MIX
MAKES 32 OUNCES, ENOUGH FOR 10 DRINKS

25 OUNCES TOMATO JUICE	1 TABLESPOON PREPARED HORSERADISH
3 OUNCES WORCESTERSHIRE SAUCE	2 TEASPOONS BLACK PEPPER
1½ OUNCES OLIVE BRINE	1 TEASPOON SALT
1 OUNCE FRESHLY SQUEEZED LEMON JUICE	1 TEASPOON CELERY SEEDS
	1 TEASPOON SRIRACHA SAUCE

Combine all of the ingredients in a large pitcher. Store in a sealed container and refrigerate for up to 3 days.

reedsburg pickling solution, aka the universal pickle brine

Simple and straightforward, pickling shouldn't have to be too fussy. Besides, one of the greatest ingredients you can ever use in pickling happens to be easy and free: time! All it takes is time for these recipes to flourish. Put on the Weezer blue album and let the good times roll. I don't care what they say about us, anyway!

Below is my universal pickling recipe, named after my hometown of Reedsburg, Wisconsin (Butter Capital of the World!). My advice: pickle each vegetable separately, don't use red wine vinegar (the color bleeds into the vegetables), and taste as you go along.

This recipe can be applied to some of the pickled vegetable garnishes used throughout the book, in recipes such as the East Indies Bloody Mary (page 128), La Boîte Bloody Maria (page 79), and Commander's Palace Bloody (page 71).

MAKES 2 CUPS

12 OUNCES DISTILLED WHITE VINEGAR

4 OUNCES WATER

1 TABLESPOON SALT

1 TEASPOON SUGAR

½ TEASPOON BLACK PEPPERCORNS

½ TEASPOON MUSTARD SEEDS

½ TEASPOON CORIANDER SEEDS

½ GARLIC CLOVE, PEELED

ASSORTED VEGETABLES FOR PICKLING

Combine the vinegar, water, salt, and sugar in a pot and bring to a boil. Once it reaches a boil, remove from the heat and let cool. Add the remaining ingredients to a 1-quart nonreactive container, ideally a mason jar. Pour the boiled vinegar contents over the spices and seasonings. Add whatever vegetable you plan on pickling.

Let rest for 24 hours before eating. A longer time to rest will improve the pickling. Unless you can your pickles following USDA guidelines, they will be perishable—I recommend storing for up to 3 weeks.

salts and infusions

If you've made your way through most of the recipes in this book, you deserve what we call in basketball parlance a lay-up. Treat yourself right. Be nice to people. And stay outta control. Like Mel Brooks always said to me, "Good to see you again, Brian. Don't be so strange."

DANER 4LIFE CHILI SALT

MAKES 1 CUP, ENOUGH
TO RIM 25 GLASSES

½ CUP SALT

½ CUP CHILI POWDER

Combine the salt and chili powder in a nonreactive sealable container. Seal the lid and shake the ingredients for 10 to 15 seconds. Store in a cool, dark place for up to 6 months.

PIMENTÓN SALT

MAKES 2½
TABLESPOONS, ENOUGH
TO RIM 14 GLASSES

1 TABLESPOON SMOKED
SWEET PAPRIKA

1 TABLESPOON SALT

½ TABLESPOON
CAYENNE PEPPER

Combine all of the ingredients in a small bowl and store in a sealed container indefinitely.

"4C" SALT

MAKES 2½
TABLESPOONS, ENOUGH
TO RIM 14 GLASSES

1 TEASPOON
CORIANDER SEEDS

1 TEASPOON
CARAWAY SEEDS

1 TEASPOON
CUMIN SEEDS

1 TEASPOON DRIED
CHAMOMILE

1 TABLESPOON SALT

Combine all of the ingredients in a spice grinder and grind to a fine powder. Store in a sealed container for up to 6 months.

153

FENNEL SALT

MAKES ½ CUP, ENOUGH TO RIM 24 GLASSES

¼ CUP FENNEL SEEDS

1½ TABLESPOONS SALT

Toast the fennel seeds in a small, dry skillet over medium heat, tossing the skillet often, for 1 to 2 minutes. Let cool. Finely grind the fennel seeds in a spice mill. Combine with the salt in a small bowl. Store in an airtight container at room temperature indefinitely.

DILL SALT

MAKES ¼ CUP, ENOUGH TO RIM 12 GLASSES

1 SPRIG DILL

¼ CUP SALT

Stir together the dill and salt in a bowl and let sit for at least 2 hours before using. Seal and store at room temperature for up to 1 month.

CHIVE AND TARRAGON SALT

MAKES 2 TABLESPOONS, ENOUGH TO RIM 10 GLASSES

1 SPRIG TARRAGON

2 FRESH CHIVES

¾ TABLESPOON SALT

¾ TABLESPOON MALDON SEA SALT

Combine all of the ingredients in a food processor and process until the herbs are finely chopped. Store in a sealed container in a cool, dark place for up to 1 month.

PEANUT-INFUSED VODKA OR TEQUILA

MAKES 12 OUNCES, ENOUGH FOR 6 DRINKS

½ CUP DRY-ROASTED PEANUTS

12 OUNCES VODKA OR BLANCO TEQUILA

Combine the peanuts and vodka in a sealed container and let sit for for 2 or 3 hours at room temperature. Pass through a fine-mesh strainer. Store in a glass bottle or a nonreactive container at room temperature for up to 6 months.

MAKES 750 ML, ENOUGH
FOR 12 DRINKS

4 STRIPS BACON

1 TABLESPOON BLACK
PEPPERCORNS

750 ML TITO'S VODKA

BACON-INFUSED VODKA

In a cast-iron skillet, cook the bacon over medium-low heat for 10 minutes. Flip the bacon and cook the other side until crispy, about 5 minutes more. The goal is to render at least 2 tablespoons of bacon fat. Remove the cooked bacon and let the bacon fat cool in the pan for a few minutes, then transfer to a container. Combine 2 tablespoons of the bacon fat and the black peppercorns in a large sealable container or mason jars with the vodka. Seal and refrigerate for 6 hours to allow the flavors to integrate. Transfer to the freezer and freeze for 30 to 60 minutes. The fat cap will look like hardened wax curdling on top of the surface. Skim off the fat cap with a big spoon and discard. Let the infused vodka come to room temperature, then pass the vodka through a fine-mesh strainer lined with cheesecloth or a coffee filter. Store in a sealed container and refrigerate for up to 3 months.

MAKES 500 ML, ENOUGH
FOR 10 DRINKS

1½ POUNDS BEETS,
PEELED AND QUARTERED

500 ML VODKA

BEET-INFUSED VODKA

Combine the beets and vodka in a sealed container and let sit for 3 days, stirring 2 or 3 times per day. After 3 days, remove the beets; be sure to use gloves, as beets can really stain your hands. Pass the vodka through a fine-mesh strainer lined with cheesecloth or a coffee filter. Store in a sealed container at room temperature for up to 6 months.

CILANTRO-INFUSED VODKA

MAKES 20 OUNCES, ENOUGH FOR 10 DRINKS

½ OUNCE OR A GOOD HANDFUL OF FRESH CILANTRO SPRIGS

20 OUNCES VODKA

Combine the cilantro and vodka in a sealed container for 24 hours. Pass through a fine-mesh strainer lined with cheesecloth or a coffee filter. Store in a sealed container at room temperature for up to 3 months.

DILL-INFUSED VODKA

MAKES 20 OUNCES, ENOUGH FOR 10 DRINKS

½ OUNCE OR A GOOD HANDFUL OF FRESH DILL SPRIGS

20 OUNCES VODKA

Combine the dill and vodka in a sealed container for 24 hours. Pass through a fine-mesh strainer lined with cheesecloth or a coffee filter. Store in a sealed container at room temperature for up to 3 months.

SHIITAKE-INFUSED VODKA

MAKES 375 ML, ENOUGH FOR 7 DRINKS

½ OUNCE DRIED SHIITAKES

375 ML POTATO VODKA

Combine the shiitakes and vodka in a mason jar or nonreactive container and let sit for 5 hours at room temperature. Pass through a fine-mesh strainer lined with cheesecloth or a coffee filter. Store in a nonreactive container for up to 6 months.

acknowledgments

Thank you, Dear Reader and Bloody Mary Enthusiast. Your ability to make your own choices and take different paths is why I am currently sending you telekinetic high fives. Creativity always deserves credit. To quote Beckett: *Ever tried. Ever failed. No matter. Try again. Fail again. Fail better.*

Most importantly, have fun when making the recipes!

Thank you to the Bloody Mary. You taught me patience. In a world full of so much intolerance, it's important to give things you don't initially like another chance to improve your mind.

Thank you to Prohibition, for ending. I'm not sure if you're directly responsible for bringing vodka and tomato juice together, but either way, thumbs up, Prohib. (Also, I'm not sure if your nickname is Prohib, but guess what, it is now.)

Thank you to Ten Speed Press for all of your wonderful support. Thank you, Emily Timberlake, for believing in me from day one and for your magical insight, steadfast guidance, and capacity to lift these pages into the stratosphere. (Additionally, thank you, Ten Speed, for providing thin enough walls in its workspace so Emily's co-workers could hear her laughing out loud while editing.) Thanks to Margaux Keres for improving the landscape on every turn of the page. Thank you, Jane Tunks Demel, for your copyediting ferocity and rocksteady correspondence. What did the drunk hippie say to the bartender who kicked him out of the bar for being wasted? "Namaste."

Thank you to Eric Medsker for your Olympian images and unyielding professionalism, and for jumping in every step of the way. Brother, you're outta sight! And thank you to Jerrie-Joy for your keen eye, kindness, and boundless support. Thank you to Ruby Taylor for providing the gush-worthy and captivating cover illustration. I am honored to share this book with y'all.

I can't step forward without praising my brother and colleague, Gabriel Stulman, and his wonderful wife Gina, who have provided me with the opportunities to work in and around the best neighborhood restaurants and bars in New York City. This book wouldn't be possible without your trust and support. I wouldn't trade either one of you for all of the peanut butter in the world! Thank you also to my business partners Matt Kebbekus and James McDuffee for being true blue, salt of the earth comrades with hearts of gold. You all inspire me. Thanks to you and your families. Thank you, Elena Silva and Leah Herman, for your unflinching support. Pop Stulman, next time I see you I promise to score you pot.

Thank you to all the Happy Cooking Hospitality investors who have provided us with the platform to serve and salute the great people of New York City and beyond. So incredibly grateful for these opportunities you have allowed us.

To all of the Happy Cooking Hospitality family, past, present, and future: thank you. Working with you is never work. It's a party! It's a song you turn up on the radio when starting a road trip. Don't ever lose the spirit you bring to each shift you work. And thank you to so many friends and regulars who visit the restaurants. You have become family and the equivalent of attending a Springsteen concert, with endless encores. Every time I see you it's a sold-out show.

A special thanks to Nick Fauchald. Any time there's a Nye's nearby, I'm buying, buddy.

Thank you to Jim Meehan for helping any and every time I asked. For those who know Jim, you know what I'm talking about. We stepped into the light together, kemosabe. Thanks for carrying the torch like Conan the Barbarian (after one thousand push-ups). Love you, buddy. Galactic high fives await thee.

HUGE thanks to Greg Boehm and Cocktail Kingdom, Robert Simonson, Stumptown Coffee, Joe Coffee, Eliot, Rob, Ted, and the Great Dane Family, the Paul's Club Family, Peter Meehan, Torina Fraboni, Allen Katz, Andrew Friedman, Chef Jin Kang, Chef Patrick McGrath, Chef Andres Trujillo, Chef Matt Griffin, Brittany "Beehave" Saliwanchik, and everyone who contributed recipes: Fernand "Pete" Petiot, Oscar Haimo, Dale DeGroff, Gary Regan, Walter Chell, Trader Vic, David Embury, Zuni Café, Nate Kinderman and the Madison Sardine Team, Shannon Ponche, Mike Henderson, Commander's Palace, Dave Sobelman, Sean Root, Sean Kenyon, Rob Krueger, Lauren Mote, Jim Meehan, Marisa and Ken Ho, Jacob Grier, Sam Parker, Kevin Denton, Leo Robitschek, Chef Jack Harris, Devon Tarby, Mark Bystrom and Jonny Hunter, Simon Ford, Kenta Goto, Matt Griffin, Farmer Lee Jones and Jamie Simpson, Ted Kilpatrick, Joseph Conklin, Craig Christopher, Kevin Patricio, Terry Alexander, Michael Rubel and The Publican, Nate Dumas, Chef Chris Lilly, Naren Young, Jeffrey Morgenthaler, Daniel Trujillo, and Gabriel Stulman. Thank you for your unwavering generosity, talents, counsel, and inspiration on the book. I'm humbled.

Thank you to my dear friends. Big Wisco. Little Wisco. World Wisco. Sam and Betsy and the Parker Family (aka the Meat Dept.), Hubes (aka Ribs Thunderpop), Quinn and Shawna, Loudest Yeller, McNeil (aka Tank Top Tommy), Mehdi and Mesh (aka Batman and Batman), Simon Kelly, Glass, Grovers, Baumanns ('sup), Tarpey (YOU take it), the San Sebastian Patricios, the Quartaros, Shim, Nashban and Amanda, Tesmer, Dermot, Dirks, Enright, Wands, Compeeeeeeee, Hirsch and Davis, Coffey, Bakopoulos and Netting, Nat and Jeremy, Madison, Reedsburg, Orlando and Donna, Welsh, Kottke, the Naces, Mahan, Marty Robbins, Kettle of Fish, y Music, Moose, McHale and Harris (aka the Duck Hardy Boys), Enjoy Yasell, and all friends near and far. Hugs and high fives will always be waiting for you.

Thank you to my family. You raised me. You still raise me. For as long as I live. Love to Mom and Dad Bartels, sisters and brothers, nieces and nephews, aunts and uncles and cousins, all of us near and far. No matter where I go, I'm still running up the stairs and through the backyard with all of you.

Lastly, thank you to all fellow bartenders, homeschooled and professional. Even you crazy whack jobs using bartending as a stepping-stone into another profession. I love learning from your mistakes and miracles, traits we all inhabit. Bartending is a sacred vocation. Treat it like a secret you can't wait to tell everyone. And holler my way if you're ever in the weeds and need a bucket of ice.

If I forgot you, I got you. Next round's on me.

. . . just waiting for the room to quiet down, so we can start the applause again. :-)

"Tell the truth. Sing with passion. Work with laughter. Love with heart. 'Cause in the end, that's all that matters."
—Kris Kristofferson

index

Published in the United States by Ten Speed Press, an imprint
of the Crown Publishing Group, a division of Penguin Random
House LLC, New York.
www.crownpublishing.com
www.tenspeed.com

Ten Speed Press and the Ten Speed Press colophon are
registered trademarks of Penguin Random House LLC.

Library of Congress Cataloging-in-Publication Data
Names: Bartels, Brian, author.
Title: The Bloody Mary : the lore and legend of a cocktail classic,
    with recipes for brunch and beyond / by Brian Bartels ;
    photography by Eric Medsker.
Description: First edition. | Berkeley : Ten Speed Press, 2017. |
    Includes bibliographical references and index.
Identifiers: LCCN 2016032143 (print) | LCCN 2016036958 (ebook)
Subjects: LCSH: Bloody Marys (Cocktails) | BISAC: COOKING
    / Beverages / Wine & Spirits. | COOKING / Beverages /
    Bartending. | COOKING / Courses & Dishes / Brunch.
Classification: LCC TX951 .B269 2017 (print) | LCC TX951 (ebook)
    | DDC 641.87/4—dc23
LC record available at https://lccn.loc.
gov/2016032143Hardcover

Hardcover ISBN: 978-1-60774-998-1
eBook ISBN: 978-1-60774-999-8

Printed in China

Design by Margaux Keres
Styling by Jerrie-Joy Redman-Lloyd

10 9 8 7 6 5 4 3 2 1

First Edition